Series / Number 07-074

EXPERIMENTAL DESIGN AND ANALYSIS

STEVEN R. BROWN
Kent State University

LAWRENCE E. MELAMED
Kent State University

SAGE PUBLICATIONS
The International Professional Publishers
Newbury Park   London   New Delhi

11-8-95

For information address:

SAGE Publications, Inc.
2455 Teller Road
Newbury Park, California 91320

SAGE Publications Ltd.
6 Bonhill Street
London EC2A 4PU
United Kingdom

SAGE Publications India Pvt. Ltd.
M-32 Market
Greater Kailash I
New Delhi 110 048 India

Printed in the United States of America

International Standard Book Number 0-8039-3854-3

Library of Congress Catalog Card No. 90-8283

95 96 97 98 99 10 9 8 7 6 5 4
Sage Production Editor: Susan McElroy

When citing a university paper, please use the proper form. Remember to cite the current Sage University Paper series title and include the paper number. One of the following formats can be adapted (depending on the style manual used):

(1) WELLER, S. C., & ROMNEY, A. K. (1990) Metric Scaling: Correspondence Analysis. Sage University Paper Series on Quantitative Applications in the Social Sciences, 07-075. Newbury Park, CA: Sage.

OR

(2) Weller, S. C., & Romney, A. K. (1990). *Metric scaling: Correspondence analysis* (Sage University Paper series on Quantitative Applications in the Social Sciences, series no. 07-075). Newbury Park, CA: Sage.

CONTENTS

SERIES EDITOR'S INTRODUCTION

Social science methods can be divided in two, nonexperimental and experimental. A key principle of experimental work is *manipulation* of a treatment variable (X), followed by observation of a response variable (Y). If I change X, and Y changes in the hypothesized way, then I am tempted to say X causes Y. However, this causal inference rests on soft ground, unless the experiment has been properly designed. Traditional experimentalists worried that the presence of other variables covarying with X might confound results. Therefore, they aimed to "hold constant" these other variables, allowing only the treatment variable to vary.

Modern experimentalists, realizing the virtual impossibility of "holding constant" all potentially relevant variables, have opted for "randomization" as a way to rule out the contaminating influence of other variables. From this perspective, Professors Brown and Melamed begin their discussion with the *completely randomized* design, the simplest version of which randomly assigns subjects to two groups, treatment and control. Consider the example of Dr. Bright, who is about to offer two courses in Psych 101. She wishes to know whether the Discussion Method of instruction (the treatment) would yield higher test scores than her usual Lecture Method (the control). Therefore, she randomly assigns the 60 students to two sections, and teaches each accordingly. Using the results from the mid-term exam (designed by a colleague ignorant of her experiment), she calculates the mean score for each section, and applies a t test. Finding the difference-of-means is not statistically significant, she tentatively concludes that the Discussion Method does not improve examination performance.

Of course, she may not rest with this preliminary assessment. Perhaps more treatment groups are needed (e.g., Team Teaching), and the application of a more general analysis of variance (ANOVA). Or, she might want to consider direct improvements in efficiency and precision. For instance, a *treatments and blocks* procedure (where, say, the students are

AUTHOR'S NOTE: *This volume was initially accepted by the former editors, Richard Niemi and John Sullivan.*

v

"stratified" into honors and nonhonors status before random assignment). Other possibilities, which may or may not be relevant for her purposes, are *repeated measures*, *hierarchical*, or *factorial* designs.

These basic designs and others are detailed in this introductory monograph, along with the appropriate statistical analysis procedures. Professors Brown and Melamed make good use of simple illustrations, for example, textbooks and student performance, perceptions of the President's ideological position. The experimental approach—for a long time the standard methodology in psychology, as well as much of education and sociology—has spread to nonexperimental bastions such as political science and economics. This volume, by its straightforward explication of a fundamental and increasingly pervasive research method, stands as a vital marker in our series.

—*Michael S. Lewis-Beck*
Series Editor

EXPERIMENTAL DESIGN AND ANALYSIS

STEVEN R. BROWN
Kent State University

LAWRENCE E. MELAMED
Kent State University

> Until there are experiments, I take no notice of anything that's done.
> (William Stephenson, 1902–1989)

1. INTRODUCTION AND OVERVIEW

In a certain sense, experimentation can be viewed as an extension of inquisitiveness, and consequently is as old as curiosity itself. There is evidence that it was beginning to take root as an organized procedure as early as the thirteenth century when the received wisdom of the Greeks was being questioned. In a more formal sense, however, the experimental method received its greatest impetus from the scientific advances of the sixteenth and seventeenth centuries, and it was because of its success that Sir Isaac Newton could confidently state that "the qualities of bodies are only known to us by experiments."

By the twentieth century, "classical" experimentation—the practice of holding everything constant except the one variable under consideration—was widely accepted in the sciences, but "modern" experimentation dates from the publication in 1935 of Sir Ronald A. Fisher's *The Design of Experiments* (see Box, 1978). According to Fisher (1960), experimentation is "experience carefully planned in advance" (p. 8), and its advantage in this respect is often attributed to its active as opposed to passive nature. Specifically, this active method consists of manipulating levels or amounts of selected independent variables (causes) to examine their influence on dependent variables (effects).

For performance on the dependent variable to be traced unambiguously to manipulated changes in the independent variable, rival sources of influence must be rendered ineffective. Under classical conditions, as noted previously, possible sources of contamination were controlled so far as possible by holding everything constant save for the experimental variable

1

(the so-called "rule of the single variable"), but the primary way in which these extraneous sources are controlled in modern experimentation is through randomization.

Suppose, for illustrative purposes, that we wished to test the comparative effectiveness of three textbooks, and so assigned one book to one class, a second to another class, and a third to yet another, as pictured in Table 1.1. If "grade on the final exam" is our performance criterion (dependent variable), then if at the end of the semester the average grade for group A is higher than those for B and C, we might be tempted to attribute that difference to the text. But if texts were assigned to preexistent groups (i.e., to groups which had been composed on a nonrandom basis), we would not really know whether the differences in final exam scores were due to the texts or to a priori group differences. Group A might have contained more seniors, for example, or greater numbers of majors than B or C, thereby biasing the outcome in favor of A: The textbook variable, in short, might be confounded with (i.e., causally inseparable from) class status, academic major, or some other variable occupying the same experimental space.

The classical solution to this uncertainty might have been to assign the texts to three groups each of which was composed of seniors and chemistry majors only, thereby neutralizing at least two important variables; for good measure, only students with average grades might be utilized in order to protect against the effect of academic achievement. Whatever the precautions, however, the classical experimenter could never wholly escape the worry that other uncontrolled contaminants might be undermining the outcome, nor could it be known whether the same results could be obtained from groups composed, say, of sophomore chemistry majors or senior mathematics majors.

But suppose that some control could be exercised over class composition, and that students could be assigned to classes on a purely random

TABLE 1.1

Text A	Text B	Text C
Student 1	Student 1	Student 1
2	2	2
3	3	3
.	.	.
.	.	.
.	.	.

basis. Each student would then have a probability of one-third of being in group A, B, or C. Assuming random assignment, Table 1.1 can be looked at anew with some confidence that class status is no longer confounded with the textbook variable; that is, under conditions of random assignment, there is no reason to expect seniors (any more than juniors, sophomores, or freshmen) to be disproportionately exposed to text A (any more than to B or C). Nor would we expect academic major or academic achievement to enter systematically into the picture.

And when one thinks about it, any and all possible variables associated with the students will be expected *in theory* to be found in roughly equal numbers across the groups: Left-handed persons should be distributed randomly among all groups, for example, and so left-handedness should in no way be in a position to bias the findings; prior education and academic achievement should have been nullified as potential contaminants; and metabolic rate, marital status of parents, number of hours of sleep the previous night, color of eyes, personality makeup, birth order, hair length—all such variables (and all others unnamed and not even conceived of) should have been neutralized through the process of randomization. What randomization succeeds in accomplishing, therefore, at least in theory, is the conversion of all irrelevant sources of possibly systematic variability into unsystematic variability, that is, into random error. The only thing that persons in group A should have in common—that is, the only source of systematic variability—is exposure to the same textbook.

Randomization procedures mark the dividing line between classical and modern experimentation and are of great practical benefit to the experimenter, as Fisher (1960: 44) noted, for they provide relief "from the anxiety of considering and estimating the magnitude of the innumerable causes by which . . . data may be disturbed," that is, from the classical difficulties of trying to hold everything constant without ever being certain that this has been achieved. Randomization has therefore been likened to life insurance inasmuch as "it is a precaution against disturbances that may or may not occur and that may or may not be serious if they do occur" (Cochran and Cox, 1957: 8). It provides no absolute guarantee, of course, but it has been judged superior to any alternative yet devised, and its possibility in experimental work is part of what distinguishes experiments, in the strict sense of the word, from quasi-experiments and surveys (see, e.g., Black, 1955; Deconchy, 1981; Martin and Sell, 1979; Selvin, 1957; Weir, 1985).

In the pages that follow, the elements of experimental design and analysis are introduced and illustrated with actual examples. It is assumed that the reader has been exposed to at least one course in basic statistics, and consequently has a nodding acquaintance with concepts such as central tendency, variability, hypothesis testing for differences between means (z and t tests), and correlation. For review purposes, and in order to establish notation to be used subsequently, the fundamental concept of variability is summarized in Chapter 2. Chapter 3 then demonstrates how variance enters into procedures for hypothesis testing, including a review of the logic of the t test for determining the statistical significance of differences between the means for two groups (experimental and control), which represents the most elementary of experimental designs. Chapter 4 shows how analysis of variance (ANOVA) is equivalent to the t test in the two-group situation, and how ANOVA can then be extended to the multigroup situation, thereby paving the way for a consideration of various experimental designs.

Experimental designs that involve the random assignment of subjects to different levels of the independent variable (i.e., to the various experimental conditions or groups) are called *completely randomized designs*. However complex these designs become, the control of extraneous influences on subjects' behavior is achieved only through randomization, and the validity of these designs in answering questions about the independent variable rests primarily on the success of the randomization procedure. These completely randomized designs are illustrated in Chapter 5.

Two potential problems with completely randomized designs concern their precision and efficiency. With regard to precision, it was noted previously that there is no absolute guarantee that randomization will keep extraneous influences in check. Were it suspected ahead of time that academic major, for example, might be an important factor in determining how a subject would perform using a particular textbook (see Table 1.1), then it might be judged wise to measure the influence of this factor directly rather than leave its control to the less certain randomization procedure. One bonus that often accrues when such extraneous factors are directly controlled is a more efficient, or powerful, statistical test of the independent variable—that is, a test more apt to detect the influence of the experimentally controlled variable—and experimental designs that control extraneous variables directly are the *treatments* × *blocks procedures* described in Chapter 7.

The problem with inefficiency arises because of the fact that completely randomized designs require the maximum number of subjects in examining questions about independent variables. From the standpoint of efficiency, it would be beneficial for a subject to participate in more than one experimental condition, thereby reducing the number of subjects required. In an examination of the influence of hours of sleep on some measure of motor performance, for example, each subject could be repeatedly tested at each level of the independent variable (hours of sleep). Such *repeated measures designs* are described in Chapter 10. It should be added that these designs also increase precision by removing extraneous variables associated with individual differences between the participants involved in the experiment. There are also designs that combine the conceptual simplicity of the completely randomized design for one or more independent variables with increasing precision and efficiency by employing a repeated measures design for one or more others. Examples of these *mixed designs* (or split-plot designs) are also given in Chapter 10.

In certain kinds of experiments it is sometimes necessary to involve several investigators in obtaining data. For example, several psychotherapists might be employed to treat clients in each segment of an experiment examining the relative efficacy of various types of psychotherapy. Any imprecisions arising from the individual characteristics of these multiple ''experimenters'' are as important to control as those contributed by the actual participants. Experimental designs that allow for such control are called *hierarchical designs* and are described in Chapter 9. Also described in Chapter 9 is the factorial design, which most often consists of combining two or more completely randomized designs into a single experiment.

Regardless of the experimental design selected, there are many statistical alternatives for determining the effectiveness of the manipulated variables. Not only can the overall effectiveness of a variable be examined, but an experimental design can be decomposed into a set of simpler ones, with analytical comparisons being performed between experimental groups in these simpler designs. This procedure—which is akin to placing the results of the original experimental design under a microscope, bit by bit—is introduced in Chapter 6 and applied to completely randomized designs, and subsequently reintroduced for use with other designs.

The question of how to select an experimental design can be answered only indirectly. A design must be structurally congruent with the research question and compatible with available resources. This monograph offers a series of plans to be judged in light of the following considerations: (1) The number of independent variables, (2) the sources and number of extraneous variables, (3) the number of subjects available for participation in the research, and (4) the questions about the independent variables that require answers. The last consideration presumes an immersion in research in one's field and knowledge of how questions are asked and what experimental designs have traditionally been used in providing answers.

In the pages that follow, unrealistically small numbers of cases are used for the sake of computational simplicity; the examples which are presented should therefore not be taken as guides beyond the principles being illustrated. Notation is likewise kept simple, with algorithms introduced in Chapter 8 to assist in conceptualizing and analyzing later and more advanced designs. Finally, treatment is restricted to experimental designs only, and the reader is referred to Spector (1981) for discussion of the broader research enterprise, field as well as experimental, of which experimentation is a part.

2. VARIABILITY

The language of science is, to a large extent, the language of variation, and experimentation is that method which seeks to explain variability by artificially effecting a change in the external world and observing the results: It is, as Machiavelli once said, the scientist's way of asking Nature a question.

By the term *variance*, statisticians are referring to the mean squared deviation around the arithmetic mean. Suppose, as an example, that four people are asked how many cups of coffee they drink per day, and that they report 3, 6, 2, and 5. The mean is therefore

$$\overline{X} = \frac{\sum X}{n}$$

$$= \frac{1}{n} \sum X$$

[2.1]

where n is the number of observations ($n = 4$ in this case), X stands for the scores that are to be summed, Σ represents the summing operation itself, $\overline{X}$ is the mean. In this particular case,

$$\overline{X} = \frac{1}{4}(3 + 6 + 2 + 5) = 4$$

It is around this mean score that variance (symbolized by S^2) is conventionally defined, according to the expression

$$S^2 = \frac{1}{n} \sum (X - \overline{X})^2$$

[2.2]

In this case,

$$S^2 = \tfrac{1}{4}[(3 - 4)^2 + \cdots + (5 - 4)^2] = 2.50$$

Variance is therefore an average (just like $\overline{X}$), that is, the average amount of squared deviation from the mean, hence its alternative name: mean squared deviation. In applications of the variance concept, the numerator of expression 2.2 is referred to as the sum of squares, or SS, and is the focus of mathematical development.

When a set of scores is selected from a larger universe of scores (i.e., when a sample is drawn from a population), the statistics which are calculated are estimates of population *parameters*: $\overline{X}$, for example, is an estimate of the parameter μ, which would be the mean number of cups of coffee consumed by all coffee drinkers, and not just those in the sample. With respect to the variance, it turns out mathematically that the best estimate of the population variance (symbolized by σ^2) is given by a modification of equation 2.2, as follows:

$$S^2 = \frac{1}{n - 1} \Sigma (X - \overline{X})^2 \qquad [2.3]$$

which, in the example of the coffee drinkers, yields

$$S^2 = (\tfrac{1}{3})(10) = 3.33$$

That the denominator in equation 2.3 is $n - 1$ rather than n reflects the fact that $\overline{X}$, which is necessary for the calculation of S^2, is itself an estimate (i.e., $\overline{X}$ is an estimate of μ); S^2 is therefore based on $n - 1$ *degrees of freedom* (df = 3), where the df represents the total number of observations minus 1 for each parameter (such as μ) that must be estimated in order to calculate the variance. Another way of expressing this is to note that with $\overline{X}$ given, as is required to calculate S^2, the sum total of all the n scores (ΣX) must also be fixed, because $\Sigma X = n\overline{X}$; therefore, if we know the value of all X scores except one, we can determine that one by subtracting the sum of all the other $n - 1$ scores from the total—that is, for any set of numbers for which the sum is known, one of those numbers is predetermined while the other $n - 1$ of them are free to vary (df = $n - 1$).

The *standard deviation* (S) is the square root of the variance, in this instance $S = \sqrt{3.33} = 1.83$. All of the squaring involved in calculating the variance is therefore compensated for by taking the square root. The standard deviation consequently expresses a kind of average deviation of all the raw scores from the mean score, that average having been weighted by the squaring operation, with the most deviant scores (when squared) carrying the greatest weight.

Equation 2.3 defines the sample variance, but for illustrative purposes below it will be convenient to employ an alternative but equivalent expression:

$$S^2 = \frac{1}{n-1}\left[\Sigma X^2 - \frac{1}{n}\left(\Sigma X\right)^2\right] \qquad [2.4]$$

In the coffee drinking example, this yields the same result as equation 2.3:

$$S^2 = \tfrac{1}{3}\left[(3^2 + \cdot \cdot \cdot + 5^2) - \tfrac{1}{4}(3 + 6 + 2 + 5)^2\right] = 3.33$$

In expressions 2.2 and 2.3, the mean score is subtracted from each raw score prior to squaring, whereas in equation 2.4 the raw scores are squared (ΣX^2) without $\overline{X}$ having first been subtracted. Expression 2.4 compensates for this by subtracting a correction factor: $CF = (1/n)(\Sigma X)^2 = 64$, which turns out to be equivalent to the mean squared n times, that is, $n\overline{X}^2 = (4)4^2 = 64$.

In the illustrations to follow, it will be convenient to simplify the statistical expressions in equation 2.4 as follows:

$$TSS = \Sigma X^2 \qquad \text{uncorrected total sum of squares}$$

$$CF = \frac{1}{n}\left(\Sigma X\right)^2 \qquad \text{correction factor}$$

$$SS_T = TSS - CF \qquad \text{corrected total sum of squares}$$

$$df = n - 1 \qquad \text{degrees of freedom}$$

Hence, the variance can be expressed as

$$S^2 = \frac{TSS - CF}{df} = \frac{SS_T}{n-1}$$

The standard deviation is therefore

$$S = \sqrt{\frac{SS_T}{n-1}}$$

The concept of statistical variability can be summarized by thinking of it as a collective expression of individual uniqueness, that is, of the extent to which persons in the same group (e.g., coffee drinkers) are dissimilar from one another, as measured by their deviation from the group average.

As will be seen, this within-group variability provides a basis for evaluating the variability that exists between groups, for example, differences between control and experimental groups.

3. *t* TEST

Experimentation at its most basic involves two groups, experimental and control, the first group typically receiving some treatment (independent variable) designed to induce an effect (dependent variable), and the second not. For purposes of illustration, suppose that members of the above group of coffee drinkers (designated group B) were observed drinking the numbers of cups reported in Chapter 2 during an experiment in which cream and sugar were available, and that four other persons comprising group A were deprived of cream and sugar.

In this illustration, the availability (group B) or unavailability (group A) of cream and sugar represents the independent variable—in this case, availability and unavailability are *levels* of the independent variable—and the number of cups of coffee consumed is the dependent variable. It is to be noted that independent variables can be either qualitative or quantitative in nature, whereas dependent variables must always be quantitative. Had the experiment included a group C in which tea as well as coffee were available, for example, then the three groups would clearly have been qualitative in character; however, had the three groups been formed around the availability of different amounts of coffee (2, 4, or 6 pitchers available to each group, say) or on the basis of group members' prior sleep deprivation (e.g., 24, 36, and 48 hours), then the groupings would have been quantitative. In either case, the dependent variable (number of cups of coffee consumed) would have been quantitative.

The results of this experiment are presented in Table 3.1, and they show that, on the average, the group with access to cream and sugar drank more cups of coffee ($\overline{X}_B = 4.00$) than the group without access to cream and sugar ($\overline{X}_A = 3.50$), and it is the magnitude of this difference ($d = 0.50$) that we wish to evaluate. This is accomplished in terms of conventional hypothesis testing, which rests on three assumptions: (1) that the population or populations sampled (coffee drinkers in this case) are normally distributed, (2) that the members of each group are obtained through random sampling techniques that insure independence of selection, and (3) that the variances within the groups are equivalent. The statistical test at issue involves the group means, and the *null hypothesis* asserts the

TABLE 3.1

Subjects	Group A	Group B
	(Cups of coffee consumed)	
1	5	3
2	3	6
3	3	2
4	3	5
Mean	3.50	4.00
S^2	1.00	3.33
S	1.00	1.83
$S_{\bar{X}}$	0.50	0.91
d	0.50	
S_d	1.04	
t	0.48	
df	6	

equivalence of the population means for which they are estimates—or, formally stated,

$$H_0: \quad \mu_A - \mu_B = 0$$

where H_0 is the null hypothesis. The alternative hypothesis, H_1, which remains viable in the event H_0 is judged untenable, is

$$H_1: \quad \mu_A - \mu_B \neq 0$$

These are two competing versions of reality, and a choice between them is made by determining the probability of H_0 being correct, a determination accomplished via the appropriate statistical test.

In choosing between H_0 and H_1, it is first necessary to evaluate the dispersion of scores within each group in order to give operational substance to the principle that

> Before it is possible to conclude with confidence that two groups are different from one another with respect to some characteristic, any difference *between* them must substantially exceed the differences *within* them with respect to that characteristic.

In the present example, therefore, were there great variability in the number of cups of coffee consumed *within* both groups A and B but very little difference *between* the average number consumed in A compared with B, it would be difficult to sustain a belief that the availability of cream and sugar is functionally important to coffee consumption.

Given that the difference in group means ($d = \overline{X}_A - \overline{X}_B$) defines the magnitude of between-group dissimilarity in performance, it remains to determine the magnitude of within-group dissimilarity in terms of which d is to be evaluated. As noted previously, the standard deviation (S) is a rough indicator of the average extent to which each individual score deviates from the group mean. S therefore applies to raw scores. A comparable expression applicable to the mean is the standard error of the mean:

$$S_{\overline{X}} = S/\sqrt{n} \qquad [3.1]$$

In the cases of groups A and B, therefore,

$$S_{\overline{X}(A)} = 1.00/\sqrt{4} = 0.50$$

$$S_{\overline{X}(B)} = 1.83/\sqrt{4} = 0.91$$

Repeated sampling from the population of coffee drinkers would produce a distribution of means, and $S_{\overline{X}}$ for the group in question is the best estimate, using that group's data, of what the standard deviation of that distribution of means would be—that is, comparable with S in relation to individual scores, $S_{\overline{X}}$ would be a rough indicator of the average amount by which each sample mean would deviate from the population mean (which is unknown).

Because the scores in each group comprise only a sample rather than the entire population, $S_{\overline{X}(A)}$ and $S_{\overline{X}(B)}$ both represent unexplained variability—that is, they are expressions of the extent, on the average, to which a group of persons who have been treated identically have inexplicably failed to behave in the same way. It is therefore permissible to merge these two conceptually equivalent figures into a single measure of collective within-group variability, which is referred to as the standard error of the difference between means:

$$S_d = \sqrt{S_{\overline{X}(A)}^2 + S_{\overline{X}(B)}^2} \qquad [3.2]$$
$$= \sqrt{0.50^2 + 0.91^2} = 1.04$$

The ratio between $d = 0.50$ (between-group difference) and $S_d = 1.04$ ("average" within-group difference) is referred to as a t test,

$$t = d/S_d \qquad [3.3]$$
$$= 0.50/1.04 = 0.48$$

and it expresses in numerical terms the principle, spelled out above, that prior to declaring two groups to be distinguishable, the explainable performance differential between the differently treated groups (numerator) must exceed the unexplainable differences among persons treated identically (denominator). How many times larger the former must be than the latter in order to be judged statistically significant is a matter of convention, and probability theory is relied upon to assess the probability of obtaining a difference as large as d if the null hypothesis is true. The smallest magnitude which a t score must reach in order for its associated mean difference to be judged significant is given in t tables for df $= n_A + n_B - 2$ and selected alpha levels (see Appendix A), where alpha (α) refers to probability levels considered too low to support the null hypothesis. In this example, df $= 4 + 4 - 2 = 6$; at $\alpha = .05$, therefore, t would have to exceed 2.45—that is, the variability between the two groups would have to be almost $2\frac{1}{2}$ times greater than the standard error before the null hypothesis could be rejected and the groups could be declared to have performed in significantly different ways.

4. ANALYSIS OF VARIANCE

The two-group t test example of the previous section is reexamined below in terms of analysis of variance (ANOVA), which is the primary statistical method employed in the univariate case, that is, in those cases in which only a single dependent variable, such as the number of cups of coffee consumed, is being appraised. (For a more detailed introduction to ANOVA, see Iversen and Norpoth, 1976; on multivariate ANOVA involving multiple dependent variables, consult Bray and Maxwell, 1986.) From the two-group case, ANOVA procedures can then be extended to greater numbers of groups and to more complex experimental situations.

The statistical decomposition effected by ANOVA is shown in Table 4.1, where the X scores in 4.1(a) are the same scores as in Table 3.1, and the scores in 4.1(b) are the raw scores squared. As specified in Chapter 2, the total sum of squared scores is designated TSS, where TSS $= 126.00$ in this case. In addition to group means—3.50 and 4.00 for groups A and B, respectively—an overall or grand mean is also calculated (GM $= 3.75$) which is the mean of all eight scores, or the mean of the two group means when $n_A = n_B$.

The scores in 4.1(c) are the original scores with GM subtracted, that is, $X - 3.75$. These are deviation scores and, by convention, are desig-

TABLE 4.1

Subjects	(a) X A	B		(b) X^2 A	B	
1	5	3		25	9	
2	3	6		9	36	
3	3	2		9	4	
4	3	5		9	25	
Sum	14	16	30	52	74	126.00 (TSS)
Mean	3.50	4.00	3.75 (GM)			

	(c) x = X − GM			(d) x^2		
1	1.25	−0.75		1.56	0.56	
2	−0.75	2.25		0.56	5.06	
3	−0.75	−1.75		0.56	3.06	
4	−0.75	1.25		0.56	1.56	
Sum	−1.00	1.00	0.00	3.25	10.25	13.50 (SS$_T$)
Mean	−0.25	0.25	0.00			

	(e) e = x − $\bar{x}$			(f) e^2		
1	1.50	−1.00		2.25	1.00	
2	−0.50	2.00		0.25	4.00	
3	−0.50	−2.00		0.25	4.00	
4	−0.50	1.00		0.25	1.00	
Sum	0.00	0.00	0.00	3.00	10.00	13.00 (SS$_e$)
Mean	0.00	0.00	0.00			

nated with the lower case x. The overall sum of Table 4.1(c) is now 0.00, and the group means have now been reduced to −0.25 and 0.25, respectively. Table 4.1(d) contains the squared deviation scores, and SS$_T$ = 13.50 is the corrected total sum of squares, that is, the total sum of squares with the effect of the grand mean taken out. As shown in Chapter 2, SS$_T$ can be calculated directly by subtracting the correction factor (CF) from TSS, where in this instance CF = $(\frac{1}{8})30^2$ = 112.50; hence, SS$_T$ = TSS − CF = 126 − 112.50 = 13.50.

Table 4.1(e) contains the x scores in 4.1(c) with the group means ($\bar{x}$) of these deviation scores subtracted. These scores are designated e (for error) and express what is unique to each subject after removal of the effects of being in the experiment itself (GM) and being in a particular experimental group ($\bar{x}$). The two columns in 4.1(e) now sum to zero, and the means ($\bar{e}$) are, of course, also zero. Table 4.1(f) contains the errors squared, the total being designated SS_e. The e^2s are therefore the same squared within-group deviations that, in Table 3.1, led to the calculation of variance. In fact, the column totals in Table 4.1(f), when divided by df = 3, are the same as the group variances in Table 3.1.

Table 4.1 breaks down the raw scores into their component parts—grand mean (GM), group mean ($\bar{x}$) after the grand mean has been removed, and individual uniqueness or error (e)—and by recombining the components, the original scores can be reconstituted, as shown in Table 4.2: GM is a constant in all scores; $\bar{x}$, the group mean, is a constant within each group, but varies in value between groups (and it is the difference between these group means which the t test evaluates); and e varies randomly both between and within groups. This demonstrates the additivity assumption of ANOVA—namely, that the total deviation of a score from the mean of all scores (GM) can be broken down into two additive components: (1) The deviation of the group mean from GM, and (2) the deviation of the particular score from the mean of its group. It is this additive sum of deviations that, when squared, produces the two component sums of squares, as shown below.

As in the case of the t test, the e values express *unexplained variability* within groups of persons treated identically, whereas the group effects (-0.25 and 0.25, respectively, $d = 0.50$) express *explainable variability* between groups of persons treated differently. In ANOVA, the former is used to evaluate the latter, as in t test expression 3.3. This is accomplished by determining how much of the total sum of squares (SS_T) is attributable to differences between groups (SS_G) as compared with differences within groups (SS_e). The relevant calculations are as follows, based on Table 4.1.

TABLE 4.2

Group A $X = GM + \bar{x}_A + e$	Group B $X = GM + \bar{x}_B + e$
$3.75 + (-0.25) + (1.50) = 5$	$3.75 + (0.25) + (-1.00) = 3$
$3.75 + (-0.25) + (-0.50) = 3$	$3.75 + (0.25) + (2.00) = 6$
$3.75 + (-0.25) + (-0.50) = 3$	$3.75 + (0.25) + (-2.00) = 2$
$3.75 + (-0.25) + (-0.50) = 3$	$3.75 + (0.25) + (1.00) = 5$
Totals	
$15.00 + (-1.00) + (0.00) = 14$	$15.00 + (1.00) + (0.00) = 16$

The total sum of squares (uncorrected) is given in 4.1(b) and is formally calculated according to the expression

$$\text{TSS} = \sum_g \sum_n X^2 \qquad [4.1]$$
$$= 5^2 + 3^2 + \cdots + 2^2 + 5^2 = 126.00$$

where Σ_n is the sum of scores across all n subjects in a group, and Σ_g is the sum of all the g group sums. However, this figure includes the effect of the overall average (GM). If there are $g = 2$ groups and $n = 4$ persons per group—and given an overall sum of 30—the correction factor for the grand mean is calculated by

$$\text{CF} = \frac{1}{gn} \left(\sum_g \sum_n X \right)^2 = (\tfrac{1}{8})30^2 = 112.50 \qquad [4.2]$$

CF is therefore equivalent to gn times the grand mean squared, that is, $\text{CF} = 8(3.75^2) = 112.50$. The corrected total sum of squares is now equal to

$$\text{SS}_T = \text{TSS} - \text{CF} \qquad [4.3]$$
$$= 126.00 - 112.50 = 13.50$$

as shown in Table 4.1(d). If there were no groups—that is, if we were merely analyzing eight ungrouped scores—the variance would be $S^2 = \text{SS}_T/\text{df} = 13.50/(8 - 1) = 1.93$.

The corrected total sum of squares is composed of the sum of squares attributable to differences between groups (SS_G) and the sum of squares attributable to differences arising within groups (SS_e), that is, $\text{SS}_T = \text{SS}_G + \text{SS}_e$. That portion of SS_T which is attributable to the differences between the groups arises in terms of the variability of the group means ($\overline{X}$) around the grand mean (GM), that is:

$$\text{SS}_G = n\left[(\overline{X}_A - \text{GM})^2 + (\overline{X}_B - \text{GM})^2\right] \qquad [4.4]$$
$$= 4\left[(3.50 - 3.75)^2 + (4.00 - 3.75)^2\right] = 0.50$$

In the above calculation, the sum of the squared deviations is multiplied by n because each group mean is based on $n = 4$ observations.

As shown in Chapter 2 (compare expressions 2.3 and 2.4), it is usually more convenient to avoid calculating deviations, and instead to use raw (uncorrected) sums and then to subtract the correction factor. The uncorrected sum of squares for groups (GSS) can be calculated using the column sums in Table 4.1(a):

$$GSS = \frac{1}{n}\left[\left(\frac{\Sigma X_A}{n}\right)^2 + \left(\frac{\Sigma X_B}{n}\right)^2\right] \qquad [4.5]$$
$$= \tfrac{1}{4}(14^2 + 16^2) = 113$$

The corrected sum of squares for groups is therefore

$$SS_G = GSS - CF \qquad [4.6]$$
$$= 113 - 112.50 = 0.50$$

And because $SS_T = SS_G + SS_e$, the latter value can be gotten through subtraction, as a residual term:

$$SS_e = SS_T - SS_G \qquad [4.7]$$
$$= 13.50 - 0.50 = 13.00$$

Alternatively, SS_e can be calculated directly from the uncorrected sums of squares:

$$SS_e = TSS - GSS \qquad [4.8]$$
$$= 126.00 - 113.00 = 13.00$$

What has been calculated so far is summarized in Table 4.3. As can be seen, $SS_G + SS_e = 13.50$ (SS_T). The sum of squares associated with the correction factor is 112.50 which, when added to the corrected total, produces TSS = 126.00, the uncorrected sum of squares. The sums of squares in the upper half of Table 4.3 are therefore independent of the mean, and it is only this information which is of experimental interest.

The degrees of freedom for within groups is obtained in the same way as in the case of the t test (Table 3.1), that is, there are $n - 1 = 3$ df for

TABLE 4.3

Source of Variance SV	Degrees of Freedom df		Corrected Sums of Squares SS	Mean Square MS	F Ratio
Between Groups	$g - 1$	$= 1$	0.50	0.50	0.23
Within Groups	$g(n - 1)$	$= 6$	13.00	2.17	
Total	$gn - 1$	$= 7$	13.50	1.93	
Grand Mean	CF	$= 1$	112.50		
Grand Total	gn	$= 8$	126.00		

each group, and $g = 2$ groups, hence $g(n - 1) = 2(3) = 6$ df. The between-group df $= g - 1 = 1$ in this case; the total df is therefore $df_G + df_e = 7$.

The *mean squares* are the sums of squares divided by their respective degrees of freedom, that is,

$$MS = SS/df \qquad [4.9]$$

hence they are variance estimates. In this case, $MS_T = SS_T/df_T = 13.50/7 = 1.93$, which would be the overall variance of these eight scores if they were ungrouped, and is therefore of virtually no interest.

$MS_e = SS_e/df_e = 13.00/6 = 2.17$, and represents the variance occurring within groups A and B combined. Compare this with the two variances in Table 3.1: As is apparent, the error mean square is merely their average, that is, $\frac{1}{2}(S_A^2 + S_B^2) = \frac{1}{2}(1.00 + 3.33) = 2.17$. MS_e in ANOVA is therefore a straightforward averaging, or pooling, of variability occurring within all groups, and is an expression of what is unexplained in the experiment.

$MS_G = SS_G/df_G = 0.50/1 = 0.50$. This reflects the average amount of variability arising from differences between groups, that is, the variability of the group means around the grand mean; therefore, this also includes the effect of the independent variable, which is explainable in terms of the design of the experiment.

MS_G and MS_e therefore stand in the same relationship as explainable to unexplainable in expression 3.3 of the t test, and in ANOVA this is given form in the F ratio:

$$F_{1,6} = MS_G/MS_e \qquad [4.10]$$
$$= 0.50/2.17 = 0.23$$

What this explainable/unexplainable ratio represents can be alternatively conceptualized in terms of the ratio between signal and noise. Had the eight subjects in Table 4.1(a) been randomly assigned to the two groups but with no experiment having taken place, this so-called "uniformity trial" would still have produced X scores indicating the number of cups of coffee consumed prior to experimental intervention; moreover, there would doubtless have been within-group variability much like that shown in the table, and it is this variability, arising because of individual differences, that constitutes the noise in the experiment. Superimposed on this background noise of uninterpretable, or random, variability in the performance of the subjects is the experimental signal, that is, the additional variability arising because of the effectiveness of the independent variable (in this case, the availability or unavailability of cream and sugar) with respect to the dependent variable (coffee consumption). If an experiment is well conducted and the independent variable truly influences behavior, the signal will be strong enough to be distinguishable from the noise, and it is this relationship that the F ratio incapsulates and appraises. What it seeks to determine, in sum, is whether there is signal variance hidden within the noise of random behavior.

Originally referred to as the variance ratio, the F ratio was given this name by George Snedecor in honor of Sir Ronald A. Fisher, and the subscripts associated with it denote the degrees of freedom for the between-group and within-group sources of variance, respectively—1 and 6 in this case. As in the case of the t test, the significance of the F ratio is determined by consulting an F table (see Appendix B), and in this instance the F table is entered in column 1 ($df_G = 1$) and row 6 ($df_e = 6$), that is, the degrees of freedom indicate where to look in the F table. Had a decision been made previously to accept as statistically significant only those mean differences that produced an F in excess of the $\alpha = .05$ tabular F value, the calculated F would have had to exceed 5.99, which it obviously does not—hence, the means of groups A and B are judged not to be significantly different.

This was the same conclusion reached using the t test, and this is necessarily so because with $g = 2$ groups, $F = t^2$: The ratio in Table 3.1 is $t = 0.48$, and $t^2 = 0.23$, which is the F ratio above. Hence, the square root of the F values in column 1 of the F table will always equal the t values from the t table for the same number of df_e and alpha level.

In the t test, with $\alpha = .05$, if the two group means are judged to be significantly different, the experimentalist theoretically runs a 5% chance of having made an erroneous judgment—that is, of having committed a *Type I error* in which a true H_0 is falsely rejected. Therefore, if the availability of cream and sugar really has no impact on the number of cups of coffee consumed, then 5% of the observed mean differences arising under repeated sampling will appear to be significant when they really are not, their apparent significance being due to the vicissitudes of sampling and other random influences. With four groups, there would be six t tests (1 vs. 2, 1 vs. 3, 1 vs. 4, 2 vs. 3, 2 vs. 4, and 3 vs. 4). In general, therefore, with g groups, there are $c = g(g - 1)/2$ comparisons, and the experimenter runs a 5% risk of making an error with each test, which means that the likelihood of making a mistake in judgment increases so that alpha no longer really describes the level of risk. With $c = 6$ comparisons and

$\alpha = .05$, for example, the level of accumulated risk is

$$\text{Risk} = 1 - (1 - \alpha)^c \qquad\qquad [4.11]$$
$$= 1 - (1 - .05)^6 = 0.26$$

Starting with the case of the t test for two groups ($c = 1$ comparison), a 5% risk quickly balloons to 26% when four groups are involved ($c = 6$). The value of ANOVA and the F test—which are equivalent to t in the two-group case—is that they can generalize the logic of the t test to cases in which $g > 2$ without increasing risk. As illustrated in subsequent sections, experiments can be designed in which significant differences among any number of groups can be detected with alpha set at any desired level.

5. COMPLETELY RANDOMIZED DESIGN

Completely randomized are the most elementary of experimental designs, and for purposes of notation will be tentatively designated CR-g (where g equals the number of groups), as suggested by Kirk (1982). (A more descriptive designation will be introduced in Section 8.1.) The design in Chapter 4, for example, was of the type CR-2, and $g = 2$ is of course the lower bound, but in principle g could extend to infinity. As noted previously, the CR design is so called because subjects are assigned randomly to experimental conditions—or, alternatively, experimental treatments are randomly applied to subjects—so that each subject initially has an identical probability of $1/g$ of being exposed to any one of the treatments.

In Table 5.1, to provide a concrete illustration, the $N = 16$ persons who agreed to participate in this experiment were blindly assigned to one of the $g = 4$ groups, those $n = 4$ persons ending up in any group being thrown together by accident. Hence, the only thing that the four subjects in group 1 have in common (at least insofar as is known) is exposure to the same experimental condition, and similarly for those in group 4. If the mean scores for those two groups differ substantially, therefore, the difference in experimental conditions is the only plausible explanation. Political party preference would be an improbable explanation, for example, because Democratic subjects are no more likely than Republican subjects to end up in either group 1 or group 4 under conditions of random assignment. And the same is true of any and all other variables—age, sex, race, personality, etc.—so that all effects except the experimental variable

TABLE 5.1

Subjects	Group 1 (3 libs)	Group 2 (2 libs)	Group 3 (1 lib)	Group 4 (0 libs)	
	(Lib/Con scores, 9 = Lib, 1 = Con)				
1	5	3	6	6	
2	3	6	5	5	
3	3	2	6	6	
4	3	5	5	7	
Sum	14	16	22	24	76 = Total sum
Mean	3.50	4.00	5.50	6.00	4.75 = GM
SS	52	74	122	146	394 = TSS
S^2	1.00	3.33	0.33	0.67	1.33 = Mean S^2

are converted into random error. And because within-group variability is an expression of all uncontrolled influences, it provides a measure of the amount of random error in the experiment, which, as demonstrated previously, can be used to evaluate the magnitude of the experimental effects.

It is to be noted, incidentally, that in this and all subsequent examples, equal ns per group are assumed. This is the goal typically sought in experimentation for reasons of computational simplicity and also because of problems that arise in the independent assessment of treatment effects in designs with more than one independent variable.

Substantively, the experimental situation that resulted in Table 5.1 consisted of subjects being instructed to evaluate President Jimmy Carter along a nine-point liberalism/conservatism continuum (1 = conservative). The experiment was conducted in February 1980, prior to the state primaries and Carter's eventual loss to Ronald Reagan. Ideology was widely believed to be a salient consideration in that election, and theoretical interest was in the salience of cognitive anchors (Rotter and Rotter, 1966), that is, in the extent to which Carter's perceived ideological position might be seen to shift under different experimental conditions. The ideological context was controlled by placing Carter's name within each of four different groups of names, as follows:

Group 1 (3 libs): Jerry Brown, Ted Kennedy, George McGovern
Group 2 (2 libs): Ted Kennedy, George McGovern, Ronald Reagan
Group 3 (1 lib): Ted Kennedy, Ronald Reagan, Gerald Ford
Group 4 (0 libs): Ronald Reagan, Gerald Ford, John Connolly

Hence, subjects in group 1 were instructed to evaluate each of four political figures—Carter plus liberals Brown, Kennedy, and McGovern—in terms of their perceived liberalism or conservatism; subjects in group 4 evaluated Carter plus conservative candidates Reagan, Ford, and Connolly. In terms of cognitive anchor theory, it was expected that Carter would be assessed as more conservative in group 1 and progressively more liberal in groups 2 through 4. The actual results are in Table 5.1.

One of the assumptions of ANOVA is that the within-group variances of the four groups are equal, that is, that they represent samples from populations with equal variances. This is the *homogeneity of variance* assumption. Some degree of difference in variance is of course to be expected because of sampling error, but this discrepancy should not be statistically significant. The variances for groups 1 through 4, as shown in Table 5.1, are 1.00, 3.33, 0.33, and 0.67, respectively. Applied to this case, a computationally simple test for homogeneity of variance is:

$$F_{max} = \frac{\text{largest } S^2}{\text{smallest } S^2} \qquad [5.1]$$

$$= \frac{3.33}{0.33} = 10.00$$

F_{max} therefore tests the equivalence of the two most discrepant variances, which are judged to be equal so long as the calculated F_{max} does not exceed the tabular F_{max} (see Appendix C). In this instance, $g = 4$ and $n - 1 = 3$ are the degrees of freedom necessary to enter the table, which shows the tabular value to be $F_{max} = 39.2$ ($\alpha = .05$), indicating that the calculated F_{max} above is well within limits. Homogeneity of variance therefore prevails, and consequently we can proceed to the analysis of variance.

The need for homogeneous variances across all groups prior to ANOVA arises from the fact that the within-group mean square, which serves as the summary expression of experimental error and which appears as the denominator of the F ratio, is itself simply the average of the g group variances, given equal group ns. (Note that the average group variance of 1.33 in Table 5.1 is the same as the error mean square in Table 5.2.) This average within-group variance can serve as a common measure of error variance for the experiment as a whole only if what is occurring errorwise in one group is essentially indistinguishable from what is occurring in every other group, so that the averaging of their variances does not, so to speak, involve mixing apples with oranges.

TABLE 5.2

SV	df	SS	MS	F
Groups	$g - 1$ = 3	17	5.67	4.25*
Error	$g(n - 1)$ = 12	16	1.33	
Total	$gn - 1$ = 15	33		

*$p < .05$

The above warning having been issued, it is nevertheless somewhat rare for variances to be heterogeneous, especially with equal ns per group. If F_{max} proves significant, however, it may be necessary, prior to performing the ANOVA, to transform the data in one of the appropriate ways described by Howell (1987: 298–305) or Kirk (1982: 79–84).

The ANOVA of the four-group data in Table 5.1 proceeds in the same manner outlined in the two-group problem of Chapter 4. Three figures are required and are obtained using expressions 4.1, 4.2, and 4.5 from the previous chapter: the uncorrected total sum of squares (TSS), the correction factor (CF), and the uncorrected sum of squares for groups (GSS). With $g = 4$ groups and $n = 4$ subjects per group, the figures are:

$$TSS = \sum_g \sum_n X^2$$
$$= 5^2 + 3^2 + \cdots + 6^2 + 7^2 = 394$$

$$CF = \frac{1}{gn}\left(\sum_g \sum_n X\right)^2$$
$$= \frac{1}{16}(76^2) = 361$$

$$GSS = \frac{1}{n}\sum_g \left(\sum_n X\right)^2 = \frac{1}{n}\left[\left(\sum_n X_1\right)^2 + \cdots + \left(\sum_n X_4\right)^2\right]$$
$$= \frac{1}{4}(14^2 + 16^2 + 22^2 + 24^2) = 378$$

The corrected sums of squares (i.e., corrected for the mean) are given as follows:

$$SS_G = GSS - CF = 378 - 361 = 17$$

$$SS_e = TSS - GSS = 394 - 378 = 16$$

$$SS_T = TSS - CF = 394 - 361 = 33$$

These same general steps apply to any completely randomized design in which there are equal numbers of subjects per group. The ANOVA summary for this experiment is summarized in Table 5.2. As before, the sums of squares for (between) Groups plus Error (within groups) add up to Total (SS_T), as do the degrees of freedom, and the general formulas for df are also the same for any completely randomized design (i.e., $g - 1$ always designates the between-group df no matter how large g is), and again assuming equal ns per experimental treatment. The mean squares, as before, are calculated by dividing each SS by its respective df. The F ratio is always calculated by MS_G/MS_e—for example, $5.67/1.33 = 4.25$ in this case. The F table (Appendix B) indicates in column 3 ($df_G = 3$) and row 12 ($df_e = 12$) that any calculated F which exceeds $F_{3,12} = 3.49$ is significant beyond the .05 level.

In this instance, a significant F indicates that at least two (and perhaps more) of the four group means are significantly different from one another; it does not tell us which means are different, however. That determination requires more detailed comparisons, such as those found in Chapter 6.

It is frequently of interest in experimental design to determine the importance of a statistical finding. Although it is known in the present case that the Groups factor is significant at a probability level less than .05 (Table 5.2), the importance or practical meaning of this result cannot be judged from the probability statement: we know only that the finding should be considered nonchance (Harcum, 1989).

There are several commonly used measures of the magnitude of a treatment effect. Perhaps the most widely used is omega-squared (ω^2), the general formula for which is

$$\omega^2 = \frac{SS_{effect} - df_{effect}MS_e}{MS_e + SS_T} \qquad [5.2]$$

where SS_{effect} and df_{effect} are associated with the treatment effect being measured. This statistic can vary from 0 to 1 (although negative values can occur when $F < 1$) and is interpreted as the proportion of the total variance in a set of data that can be accounted for or explained by the experimental factor. It should be pointed out that this formula is for the most common design situation, that is, one in which the treatment variable is a "fixed" factor (see Chapter 8 for the distinction between fixed and random effects).

For the findings in Table 5.2, expression 5.2 yields

$$\omega^2 = \frac{SS_G - (g - 1)MS_e}{SS_T + MS_e}$$

$$= \frac{17 - (3)1.33}{33 + 1.33} = 0.38$$

Interpretations of ω^2 usually follow Cohen (1977), who suggests that a large effect has an $\omega^2 \geq 0.15$, a medium effect about 0.06, and a small effect 0.01. The above finding of a significant Groups effect would have to be considered large because 38% of the variance in the data can be accounted for by knowing the ideological context group to which subjects belong.

An excellent discussion of ω^2 can be found in Keppel (1982: 89–96). Howell (1987) gives a thorough account of alternatives, such as eta-squared and the squared intraclass correlation coefficient. O'Grady (1982) offers a well-reasoned critique of the use of measures of strength of an effect in the ANOVA.

6. COMPARISONS AND TRENDS

Performing an ANOVA on the data of a particular design may appear to represent a necessary and sufficient course of action for detecting the effectiveness of experimental manipulations, but this is not the case on either account. In order to understand why, however, it is helpful to think of an experimental design as a construction that can be built of several components; conversely, it can also be conceived as one that can be broken down or decomposed into its constituent parts.

The CR design of the previous chapter, for example, can be thought of as being composed of several alternative *comparisons* between different ideological context groups. An alternative to performing an overall ANOVA involving all the groups in the CR design would therefore be to examine one or more comparisons that involve some subset of the groups. Thus it may really only be of interest to see if there is a significant difference between group 4 (no liberals) and each of the other three groups, and this set of three comparisons could be used instead of the overall ANOVA. On the other hand, there may be only one comparison that is of interest, for example, the average of the means of groups 1, 2, and 3 versus group 4's mean. This is a "complex" comparison whereas the group versus group comparisons are denoted as "simple" or "pairwise" comparisons. The F statistic, in actuality, is a simultaneous test of all possible simple and complex comparisons involving the same groups. If F is significant, then there is some comparison that would also be significant. The problem is to identify it.

So far, reasons have been given for not considering an overall ANOVA as a necessary mode of analysis for any particular design. The reason it is also not likely to be sufficient is that the overall ANOVA generally answers questions that are only preliminary or broadly focused, that is, that lead to more specific inquiries. Consequently, many investigators will perform an overall ANOVA on a CR design, and most other designs as well, but will follow it with a set of comparisons. For instance, it may be theoretically important for a researcher to be able to state that ideological context is a significant influence on voting behavior, but this same researcher may also have a need to know if it is as effective with a weak anchor (as in group 3) as it is with a strong anchor (group 1).

6.1. A Priori Comparisons

When comparisons are established before an experiment is executed, they are termed *a priori* or *planned*, and are usually driven by previous research findings and/or theoretical considerations. Before conducting the experiment on ideological context, for example, interest may have centered on determining whether the extreme cases might at least be significantly different—that is, in learning whether evaluations of Carter's liberalism were altered depending on whether his name appeared with three liberals and no conservatives (group 1) or with three conservatives and no liberals (group 4). This would mean ignoring groups 2 and 3, and this is symbolized in row $C1$ of Table 6.1, which contains the group totals (G) from Table 5.1 plus the lambda (λ) coefficients that are used to define the comparisons. The coefficients for planned comparison $C1$, when multiplied by the group totals, will have the effect of canceling out groups 2 and 3 and determining the magnitude of difference between groups 1

TABLE 6.1

Planned Comparisons	Groups					
	1	*2*	*3*	*4*		
	Group Totals (G)				$\Sigma\lambda$	$\Sigma\lambda^2$
	14	16	22	24		
$C1$: 1 vs. 4	1	0	0	-1	0	2
$C2$: 2 vs. 3	0	1	-1	0	0	2
$C3$: 1, 4 vs. 2, 3	$\frac{1}{2}$	$-\frac{1}{2}$	$-\frac{1}{2}$	$\frac{1}{2}$	0	1
$C1 \times C2$	0	0	0	0	0	
$C1 \times C3$	$\frac{1}{2}$	0	0	$-\frac{1}{2}$	0	
$C2 \times C3$	0	$-\frac{1}{2}$	$\frac{1}{2}$	0	0	

and 4, namely:

$$\sum \lambda G = (1)(14) + (0)(16) + (0)(22) + (-1)(24)$$
$$= 14 - 24 = -10$$

The set of lambda coefficients is considered legitimate if $\sum \lambda = 0$, which is the case for $C1$. It will be noted that when this is true, there is always a specific difference being examined—namely, that between the group (or groups) whose data are weighted by positive coefficients and those whose data are weighted by negative coefficients. Note also that $\sum |\lambda|$, that is, the sum of the absolute values for this set of coefficients, is 2. Whereas this is not a requirement for legitimacy, it is a convenient situation for complex comparisons such as $C3$, as will be seen.

In general the corrected sum of squares attributable to a comparison is given by the expression:

$$SS_C = \frac{\left(\sum \lambda G \right)^2}{n \sum \lambda^2} \qquad [6.1]$$

where in this case $\sum \lambda G = -10$, as calculated above; $n = 4$ persons per group; and $\sum \lambda^2 = 2$ (see Table 6.1). Hence:

$$SS_{C1} = \frac{(-10)^2}{(4)(2)} = 12.5$$

Comparison $C2$ in Table 6.1 pits group 2 against group 3:

$$SS_{C2} = \frac{\left[(0)(14) + (1)(16) + (-1)(22) + (0)(24) \right]^2}{(4)(2)}$$
$$= \frac{(-6)^2}{8} = 4.5$$

Comparison $C3$ focuses on combined groups and as such is a complex comparison. Here the average performance of groups 1 and 4 combined is compared with that of groups 2 and 3:

$$SS_{C3} = \frac{\left[(\tfrac{1}{2})(14) + (-\tfrac{1}{2})(16) + (-\tfrac{1}{2})(22) + (\tfrac{1}{2})(24) \right]^2}{(4)(1)}$$
$$= \frac{(19 - 19)^2}{4} = 0$$

The number of planned comparisons to be made and the manner in which the corrected sums of squares associated with them are to be evaluated depends on whether or not these comparisons are *orthogonal*. When comparisons are orthogonal, they are independent, the information used in one comparison being different from that used in another. The number of orthogonal planned comparisons is constrained by the between-groups degrees of freedom. For the experimental design of Table 6.1, $g - 1 = 3$ represents the size of the set of orthogonal comparisons, and $C1$, $C2$, and $C3$ are the three members of this set. In order to establish that a pair of comparisons is orthogonal, it is necessary to cross multiply their lambda coefficients, that is, to multiply the first coefficient of $C1$ by the first coefficient of $C2$, and so forth for the other pairs of coefficients. When the sum of cross products is zero, the comparisons are orthogonal. Thus, $C1$ and $C2$ are orthogonal because $\Sigma(\lambda_{C1}\lambda_{C2}) = (1)(0) + (0)(1) + (0)(-1) + (-1)(0) = 0$.

The value of restricting comparisons to an orthogonal set is in the maintenance of Type I error control. Recall that in performing an ANOVA, the probability of rejecting H_0 when it is in fact true (i.e., a Type I error) is restricted, typically, to $\alpha = .05$. When a set of comparisons is conducted, however, there is the possibility of a Type I error occurring in any one of them. Ordinarily, the concept of a Type I error rate must be considered *familywise*—that is, the probability of at least one Type I error for the set or family of comparisons, a matter to be addressed in greater detail subsequently. For the moment, it is sufficient to acknowledge that orthogonal comparisons escape such concern because they involve independent pieces of information. What are essentially being conducted are separate, stand-alone ANOVAs that do not constitute some higher-order entity or family.

Consider the independent ANOVAs for the set of orthogonal comparisons in Table 6.1. First note that it makes good theoretical sense to compare the most extreme groups 1 and 4 (comparison $C1$), and an investigator might even mount a case for studying any fine difference between middle groups 2 and 3 ($C2$); however, comparing the average of groups 1 and 4 with that of 2 and 3 ($C3$), although making no obvious sense theoretically, is forced on the investigator by virtue of the prior choice of $C1$ and $C2$—that is, with $C1$ and $C2$ specified, $C3$ is the only remaining comparison that will complete an orthogonal set.

The sums of squares for a set of orthogonal comparisons add up to the between-groups sum of squares for that variable, as shown in Table 6.2—that is, SS_G has been decomposed into the three components represented

TABLE 6.2

SV	df	SS	MS	F
Groups	3	17.00	5.67	4.25**
(C1)	(1)	(12.50)	12.50	9.38***
(C2)	(1)	(4.50)	4.50	3.38*
(C3)	(1)	(0.00)	0.00	0.00
Error	12	16.00	1.33	
Total	15	33.00		

$*p < .10, **p < .05, ***p < .01$

by the orthogonal comparisons: $SS_G = SS_{C1} + SS_{C2} + SS_{C3} = 12.50 + 4.50 + 0.00 = 17.00$. Likewise, $df_G = 3$ has also been decomposed, with 1 df going to each comparison. The F ratio for the Groups effect remains the same as reported previously. The F ratios for the comparisons ($F = MS_C/MS_e$) are compared with $F_{1,12}$ from Appendix B. The large F for C1 indicates that the difference between the group 1 and 4 means is highly significant ($p < .01$); the F for C2 is significant at $p < .10$ (an alpha level best used only for exploratory research); F for C3 is not significant.

It is important to point out that the set of orthogonal comparisons used in Table 6.1 is not the only possible set. For example, consider C', an alternative set of lambda coefficients that are also orthogonal:

$$C1': \quad 1 \quad -1 \quad 0 \quad 0 \qquad SS_{C1'} = 0.50 \quad (F = .38)$$

$$C2': \quad 0 \quad 0 \quad 1 \quad -1 \qquad SS_{C2'} = 0.50 \quad (F = .38)$$

$$C3': \quad \tfrac{1}{2} \quad \tfrac{1}{2} \quad -\tfrac{1}{2} \quad -\tfrac{1}{2} \qquad SS_{C3'} = 16.00 \quad (F = 12.03, p < .01)$$

Which of several possible sets of orthogonal contrasts is constructed depends on which comparisons are deemed to be of a priori importance by the experimenter, who cannot examine more than one set and still use the procedures introduced above for evaluating the significance of the resulting F ratios.

6.2. The Dunn Test

In the event that the a priori or planned comparisons of interest are greater in number than $g - 1$ and/or are not orthogonal to each other, the most common strategy is to use the *Dunn multiple comparison test*, which is based on the *Bonferroni inequality*. The latter expresses the relationship between the alpha level (probability of a Type I error) per comparison (α_{pc}) and the alpha level familywise (α_{fw}), namely: $\alpha_{fw} \leq \Sigma\alpha_{pc}$. The implication of this inequality is that α_{fw} can be divided among the members of the set of comparisons. This new α_{pc} level is then used for testing the significance of each comparison. In this way, α_{fw} can be maintained no matter how many comparisons are involved. Consider the specific example in which there are four comparisons. Here, α_{pc} would be set at .0125 (i.e., $\alpha_{fw}/4$), and, given the Bonferroni inequality, we would be certain that α_{fw} is not greater than .05 (i.e., 4 × .0125) for the set of four comparisons.

An obvious question that arises is, Where are F or t values to be found for alpha levels such as .0125? Fortunately, the table used with the Dunn test (see Appendix E) incorporates the adjustment of α_{pc} for each particular number of comparisons, and simply requires looking up a critical value for that particular number of comparisons and df_e .

Rather than the F of the ANOVA, the Dunn test employs a t statistic, a particularly useful version of which is:

$$t = \frac{C_a\overline{X}_a + C_b\overline{X}_b + \cdots + C_p\overline{X}_p}{\left[MS_e(C_a^2/n_a + \cdots + C_p^2/n_p)\right]^{1/2}} \qquad [6.2]$$

This formula can be used for both simple and complex comparisons, as well as in situations in which the groups do not have equal numbers of subjects. When only pairwise comparisons are to be made and both groups have the same number of subjects, the formula simplifies to:

$$t = \frac{C_a\overline{X}_a + C_b\overline{X}_b}{\sqrt{2MS_e/n}} \qquad [6.3]$$

In both formulas, each C represents a coefficient for a comparison, each $\overline{X}$ represents a group mean that will be multiplied by that coefficient, n is the number of scores in each group, and MS_e is the error mean square taken from the ANOVA analysis.

Assume that the two planned comparisons of greatest interest from the ideological context study are (1) a comparison of groups 1 and 4, and (2) a comparison involving the average of groups 1, 2, and 3 in contrast to the performance of group 4. The coefficients defining the first comparison ($C1$) are 1 0 0 −1, whereas those defining the second ($C2$) are $\frac{1}{3}$ $\frac{1}{3}$ $\frac{1}{3}$ −1. The $C1 \times C2$ sum of cross products is $1\frac{1}{3}$, indicating that these two comparisons are not orthogonal. Table 6.3 contains the means for the

TABLE 6.3

	Group Means				
	1	2	3	4	
	3.5	4.0	5.5	6.0	Sum
C1	1	0	0	-1	0
C2	$\frac{1}{3}$	$\frac{1}{3}$	$\frac{1}{3}$	-1	0
C1 $\times$ C2	$\frac{1}{3}$	0	0	1	$1\frac{1}{3}$

four ideological context groups. The final piece of information required is found in Table 6.2: $MS_e = 1.33$, $df_e = 12$.

From a Dunn's table (Appendix E), it is determined that when the number of comparisons is $c = 2$, $\alpha_{fw} = .05$, and $df_e = 12$, the t_D required for rejecting H_0 is 2.56. (It should be clear from the previous discussion that each comparison is actually being tested with $\alpha = .025$.) Using expression 6.3 and computing t_D for $C(1)$:

$$t_D = \frac{(1)(3.5) + (-1)(6.0)}{\sqrt{(2)(1.33)/4}}$$

$$= -3.06$$

which allows the rejection of H_0. (Because the test is two-tailed, the direction of the difference between groups 1 and 4 is irrelevant.)

For $C(2)$, expression 6.2 is employed:

$$t_D = \frac{(\frac{1}{3})(3.5) + (\frac{1}{3})(4.0) + (\frac{1}{3})(5.5) + (-1)(6.0)}{\left\{1.33\left[(\frac{1}{3})^2/4 + (\frac{1}{3})^2/4 + (\frac{1}{3})^2/4 + (-1)^2/4\right]\right\}^{1/2}}$$

$$= \frac{4.33 - 6.00}{\sqrt{(1.33)(.33)}} = -2.50$$

which is not significant.

It is advisable to restrict usage of Dunn's test to as small a set of planned comparisons as possible, the reason being that α_{pc} is inversely proportional to the number of comparisons made. When the number of comparisons is large and, therefore, an extremely small alpha is used—for example, .005 for 10 comparisons and α_{fw} at .05—the probability of *Type II errors* will be very high; that is, it will be increasingly difficult to reject H_0 when it is false.

Extended discussions of the Dunn test can be found in Marascuilo and Serlin (1988). Keppel (1982) offers a useful modification of the Dunn-Bonferroni strategy for large sets of comparisons.

6.3. Trend Analysis

The raw data in Table 5.1 are *quantitative* in nature, that is, the experimental contrivance involved reducing the number of liberals with whom Jimmy Carter's name appeared; moreover, it also involved a known interval, each group (after group 1) being decreased by one liberal figure. These two features, quantitative data and intervals of known size, permit the analysis of trends.

The trends for which any data set can be tested are a function of the number of degrees of freedom for Groups: In this case, there are $g - 1 = 3$ trends, as shown in Figure 6.1. If the data behave in a linear fashion (L), then estimations of Jimmy Carter's liberalness will show a progressive increase or decrease as the number of conservative names increases. If the data behave quadratically (Q), there will be a drop followed by a subsequent rise, or vice versa; that is, there will be one change of direction in the trend. Cubic data (C) will change directions twice. The actual data configuration in this case also appears in Figure 6.1.

L, Q, and C are orthogonal polynomials which express these trends numerically, and the sums of squares for trends can be calculated using the same expression as 6.1 above, namely

$$SS_{trend} = \frac{\left(\sum \lambda G\right)^2}{n \sum \lambda^2} \qquad [6.4]$$

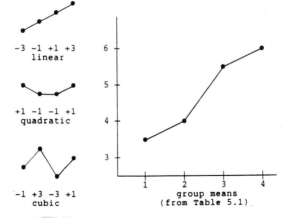

Figure 6.1.

TABLE 6.4

| Trends | Groups | | | | $\Sigma\lambda$ | $\Sigma\lambda^2$ |
	1	2	3	4		
	Group Totals (G)					
	14	16	22	24		
L	−3	−1	1	3	0	20
Q	1	−1	−1	1	0	4
C	−1	3	−3	1	0	20

where G is the group total. (The λs in equation 6.4 are different from those in equation 6.1, and can be found in specialized tables for trend analysis located in advanced texts, e.g., Kirk, 1982.) The relevant data are in Table 6.4, and the computations are as follows:

$$SS_L = \frac{[(-3)(14) + \cdots + (3)(24)]^2}{(4)(20)} = 16.20$$

$$SS_Q = \frac{[(1)(14) + \cdots + (1)(24)]^2}{(4)(4)} = 0.00$$

$$SS_C = \frac{[(-1)(14) + \cdots + (1)(24)]^2}{(4)(20)} = 0.80$$

The ANOVA summary in Table 6.5 reveals that only the linear trend is significant ($p < .01$)—that is, as anchor theory would predict, estimations of Jimmy Carter's liberalness varied linearly (and positively) with increases in the number of conservative figures with whom he was com-

TABLE 6.5

SV	df	SS	MS	F
Groups	3	17.00	5.67	4.25*
L	(1)	(16.20)	16.20	12.15**
Q	(1)	(0.00)	0.00	0.00
C	(1)	(0.80)	0.80	0.60
Error	12	16.00	1.33	
Total	15	33.00		

*$p < .05$, **$p < .01$

pared, although, as will be shown, only the means of the first and fourth groups are actually significantly different. In sum, the trend is marked although the actual group differences are modest.

It is worth noting that of the trend sums of squares in Table 6.5, the linear trend accounts for $16.20/17.00 = 0.95$ (95%) of the Groups sum of squares, the square root of which is a correlation ($r = 0.98$), which expresses the relationship between the linear polynomial (L) and the group totals in Table 6.4.

6.4. A Posteriori Comparisons

It is not always the case that an experimenter knows beforehand what comparisons will be worth evaluating. Many times, comparisons are suggested by the fact that a significant F was obtained and the researcher desires to know more about the source of this result. Perhaps hypotheses about the independent variable came to mind only after conducting the experiment. These *a posteriori* or *unplanned* comparisons can greatly increase the probability of Type I errors (i.e., inflate α_{fw}) because they are often large in number, use nonindependent sources of information, and are based on knowledge already gained via the ANOVA. There are many specific tests for unplanned comparisons, only two of which will be described here: the Tukey HSD (Honestly Significant Difference) test for simple (pairwise) comparisons and the Scheffé test for complex ones.

Tukey HSD Test. The HSD test uses the Studentized range distribution rather than the t or F distribution. Ordinarily a table is created, such as Table 6.6, in which the group means are ranked in order and all differences between these means are calculated. In Table 6.6, it can be seen that the largest difference between means is 2.5, and this difference

TABLE 6.6

		Group Means		
	4	3	2	1
	6.0	5.5	4.0	3.5
4	—	0.5	2.0	2.5*
3		—	1.5	2.0
2			—	0.5
1		$S_{\bar{X}} = 0.58$		—

*$p < .05$

involves a range spanning four ordered means. This information is necessary for performing the HSD test.

The Studentized range distribution appears in Appendix D, and its critical value, labeled q, is obtained by entering the table with α_{fw}, df_e, and r (range), the latter being the number of places, or "steps," between the two most extreme of the ordered means. For Table 6.6, with $r = 4$, $df_e = 12$, and $\alpha_{fw} = .05$, the critical value of q is 4.20.

The statistic q is similar to t and, in fact, differs only by a constant value of $\sqrt{2}$. q_{HSD} can be computed for each of the six differences in Table 6.6 by using the formula:

$$q_{HSD} = \frac{\overline{X}_i - \overline{X}_j}{\sqrt{S_{\overline{X}}}} \qquad [6.5]$$

where $\overline{X}_i$ and $\overline{X}_j$ are any two means and $S_{\overline{X}}$ is the standard error of the mean, which, in turn, is equal to $\sqrt{MS_e/n}$, where MS_e is from the ANOVA (Table 6.2, $MS_e = 1.33$) and n is group size ($n = 4$ in this case).

For the comparison of groups 1 and 4,

$$q_{HSD} = \frac{2.50}{\sqrt{1.33/4}} = 4.33$$

which is significant ($p < .05$), because it exceeds the critical value of 4.20.

The other five comparisons can now be conducted, but it is easier to use a "critical difference" approach for all six comparisons, because with this procedure only one computation is required, that being the minimum difference that must exist between *any* pair of means in order to reject H_0. This critical difference (CD) value, which can be used simultaneously to examine all entries in Table 6.6, is calculated as follows:

$$CD_{HSD} = q_{r,\alpha,df_e}\sqrt{MS_e/n} \qquad [6.6]$$

where q is from the Studentized range for $r = 4$, $\alpha = .05$, and $df_e = 12$, as determined previously, and equals 4.20. Similarly, $\sqrt{MS_e/n} = .58$; therefore, $CD_{HSD} = (4.20)(.58) = 2.44$. In examining Table 6.6, only the difference between groups 1 and 4 is large enough to be significant, that is, only $d = 2.50$ exceeds $CD = 2.44$.

Tukey's HSD test works by maintaining α_{fw} for the entire set of pairwise comparisons. This widely researched test is discussed at length in Kirk (1982). It should be noted that there are alternative versions of this test for designs with unequal group sizes. One peculiarity of the Tukey procedure bears mentioning—namely, that a significant overall F can be obtained when no pairwise comparisons prove significant. One possible reason for this apparent anomaly is that the critical comparisons may be complex rather than the simple ones evaluated by the Tukey test.

Scheffé Test. For complex comparisons, the most widely employed test for unplanned or post hoc comparisons is the Scheffé, which uses the F distribution where the critical difference is obtained employing the following formula:

$$\text{CD}_\text{S} = \sqrt{(g-1)F_{\alpha;\,df_1,\,df_2}}\ \sqrt{\text{MS}_e \sum (C^2/n)} \qquad [6.7]$$

In this equation, g refers to the number of groups, $F_{\alpha;\,df_1,\,df_2}$ is the critical value from the F table (Appendix B) for that alpha and those numerator and denominator degrees of freedom, MS_e is from the overall ANOVA, C represents a member of the set of coefficients that defines the comparison, and n is group size.

To demonstrate the Scheffé test, a comparison between the average performance of groups 1 and 2 and that of groups 3 and 4 of the ideological context study will be examined. The set of lambda coefficients is $\frac{1}{2}\ \frac{1}{2}\ -\frac{1}{2}\ -\frac{1}{2}$, and the obtained difference, using the means from Table 6.6, is $\frac{1}{2}(4.0 + 3.5) - \frac{1}{2}(6.0 + 5.5) = -2.0$. The critical difference is calculated using expression 6.7 as follows, there $g = 4$, $F_{.05;\,3,\,12} = 3.49$, $\text{MS}_e = 1.33$, and $n = 4$:

$$\text{CD}_\text{S} = \sqrt{(3)(3.49)}\ \sqrt{(1.33)\big\{\big(\tfrac{1}{2}\big)^2/4 + \cdots + \big(-\tfrac{1}{2}\big)^2/4\big\}}$$

$$= (3.24)\ \sqrt{1.33(4)(\tfrac{1}{16})} = 1.87$$

The obtained difference of 2.00 (the minus is irrelevant) exceeds the critical value of 1.87, and this difference between groups 1 and 2 versus groups 3 and 4 is therefore significant ($p < .05$).

There are two factors to keep in mind in using the Scheffé test. First, if the overall F is not significant, then no significant comparison can be found, and it would be unprofitable to conduct the Scheffé test under these circumstances. Second, it is plain from the CD_S formula that this test could also be used for pairwise unplanned comparisons; this would not be wise, however, because Scheffé's is the most conservative of all tests that are available for that purpose, and produces an unacceptably high level of Type II errors.

There is a vast literature on comparison procedures and many specialized texts exist. The discussions by Keppel (1982), Kirk (1982), and

Klockars and Sax (1986) are especially thorough. A valuable advanced treatment of this topic is in Wilcox (1987). Of special importance are procedures to be employed when certain assumptions of the ANOVA are violated, such as the requirement for homogeneous variances.

7. TREATMENTS BY BLOCKS

The randomized block design, or the treatments by blocks design as it is increasingly referred to, is a modification of the completely randomized design that takes into a priori account the possible effect of a *nuisance variable* on the dependent variable. A nuisance variable is one in which there is no experimental interest, but one which, if left unattended, is of sufficient potential danger to the integrity of the experiment that it is considered risky simply to cross one's fingers and hope that its effect will be nullified by the process of random assignment.

In terms of the hypothetical experiment in Table 1.1, as an example: Were there some concern that the most able students might end up in group A and the least able in C—such that subsequent exam performance (dependent variable) might have nothing to do with the relative virtues of the textbooks (independent variable), but with an irrelevant characteristic (i.e., nuisance variable) of the exam takers—then this possibility might be effectively neutralized by randomly assigning the three students with the highest grade averages (block 1) to groups A, B, and C; the three with the next-highest grade averages (block 2) likewise randomly to A, B, and C; etc. In this way, all three groups would in equal measure contain students with the highest and lowest abilities.

The treatments by blocks design is available for situations in which there is a single nuisance variable that is deemed necessary to control on an a priori basis, and for purposes of notation it will tentatively be designated TB-gb, where g stands for the number of treatment groups (as in the CR-g design) and b represents the number of blocks into which the nuisance variable has been divided.

To provide a concrete illustration: In Chapter 5, it was reported that the study of President Carter's perceived liberalism was conducted by gathering 16 persons and assigning them randomly to the four treatment groups; suppose, however, that the data were collected with the assistance of four interviewers, each of whom was instructed to administer the test to four acquaintances. Had this been the case, then the test materials in the possession of each interviewer would have included one administration for each of the $g = 4$ experimental conditions, which would have

TABLE 7.1

Blocks	Group 1 (3 libs)	Group 2 (2 libs)	Group 3 (1 lib)	Group 4 (0 libs)	Sum
Interviewer	(Lib/Con scores, 9 = Lib, 1 = Con)				
1	5	3	6	6	20
2	3	6	5	5	19
3	3	2	6	6	17
4	3	5	5	7	20
Sum	14	16	22	24	76 = Grand sum
Mean	3.50	4.00	5.50	6.00	4.75 = GM

been given to four interviewees on a random basis. For illustrative purposes, the raw scores in Table 7.1 are the same as those in Table 5.1, but the analysis below is somewhat different in order to take into account the above restriction in subject assignment.

In Table 7.1, there is a possibility that something systematic might occur in the rows of the design because of the personal predilections and circumstances of the interviewers. In this connection, the interviewer effect is a nuisance variable of no interest insofar as this particular experiment is concerned, but is a potential source of additional noise which could drown out the signal from the variable of interest (i.e., estimates of Carter's liberalism under the four group conditions) and which will remain disguised as random error if not taken into account. It is the purpose of the TB design to obtain an estimate of the impact of the blocks (interviewers) and to remove it from the error estimate.

The analysis proceeds much as demonstrated in Chapters 4 and 5 for calculating the uncorrected total sum of squares (TSS), the correction factor (CF), and the uncorrected sums of squares for groups (GSS). With $g = 4$ groups and $b = 4$ blocks (the fact that $g = b$ is incidental), and where Σ_g and Σ_b designate summation over groups and blocks, respectively, the calculations are as follows:

$$TSS = \sum_g \sum_b X^2 = 5^2 + 3^2 + \cdots + 6^2 + 7^2 = 394$$

$$CF = \frac{1}{gb}\left(\sum_g \sum_b X\right)^2 = \tfrac{1}{16}(76)^2 = 361$$

$$GSS = \frac{1}{b}(G_1^2 + \cdots + G_4^2) \quad \text{where } G = \text{group sum }\left(\text{or } \sum_b X\right)$$

$$= \tfrac{1}{4}(14^2 + 16^2 + 22^2 + 24^2) = 378$$

The uncorrected sum of squares for blocks (BSS) is calculated in the same way as GSS, but for the rows; that is, the row totals are squared and then divided by the number of observations ($g = 4$) that entered into the sum:

$$\text{BSS} = \frac{1}{g}(B_1^2 + \cdots + B_4^2) \quad \text{where } B = \text{block sum} \left(\text{or } \frac{\sum X}{g}\right)$$
$$= \tfrac{1}{4}(20^2 + 19^2 + 17^2 + 20^2) = 362.50$$

The corrected sums of squares for groups, blocks, and total are calculated as follows and are entered in Table 7.2:

$$\text{SS}_G = \text{GSS} - \text{CF} = 378 - 361 = 17$$
$$\text{SS}_B = \text{BSS} - \text{CF} = 362.5 - 361 = 1.5$$
$$\text{SS}_T = \text{TSS} - \text{CF} = 394 - 361 = 33$$

The error sum of squares is simply a residual—that is, the sum of squares that remains after the group and block effects have been accounted for—and so can be calculated by subtraction:

$$\text{SS}_e = \text{SS}_T - \text{SS}_G - \text{SS}_B = 33 - 17 - 1.5 = 14.50$$

As in the case of the CR-g design, $\text{MS} = \text{SS}/\text{df}$, and the F ratio is formed by dividing MS_e into MS_G and MS_B, respectively. It is to be noted that the general formulas for degrees of freedom will be the same for all randomized block designs of this type (i.e., in which there is one observation in each group-block cell), although the size of both g and b will vary from study to study.

Because of blocking and the potentially correlated row errors to which it gives rise, the F for blocks, as calculated above, may not be appropriate; this is of little consequence, however, because there is normally no interest in testing blocks, only the groups—that is, in this case, interviewer differences are a nuisance variable, which it was deemed necessary a priori to control, but not to test as a variable of experimental interest.

TABLE 7.2

SV	df			SS	MS	F
Groups	$g - 1$	=	3	17.00	5.67	3.52
Blocks	$b - 1$	=	3	1.50	0.50	0.31
Error	$(g - 1)(b - 1)$	=	9	14.50	1.61	
Total	$gb - 1$	=	15	33.00		

The $F = 3.52$ for groups is significant at only the $\alpha = .10$ level when compared with the tabular F (for $df_G = 3$ and $df_e = 9$), which is below the conventional .05 level; group differences would therefore typically be regarded as not significant, which would preclude the a posteriori testing of group means. On the other hand, if a priori comparisons have been planned, they can be tested using the same procedures described in Chapter 6, but with MS_e and df_e as specified for the TB design. Similarly with respect to trend tests: The linear trend in the CR case in Chapter 6 was significant, and the same trend in the TB case yields significance also ($p < .05$).

The reason for the reduction in significance of the Groups effect in the case of the TB design (compared with the CR design) can be explained in terms of Figure 7.1. In the case of both designs, SS_G is the same; what is different is the magnitude of the error term, which, as the denominator of the F ratio, directly influences whether or not F reaches a significant level. As shown in Figure 7.1, SS_e in the CR design is divided into two parts in the TB design: SS_B and SS_e. But the degrees of freedom are also divided: $df_e = 12$ in the CR design are divided into $df_B = 3$ and $df_e = 9$ in the TB design. Although SS_e is diminished in the TB design, therefore, and although this could reduce MS_e (hence increase the significance of F), the df_e are also diminished to an even greater extent. Consequently, MS_e is actually increased, and the F ratio is thereby reduced.

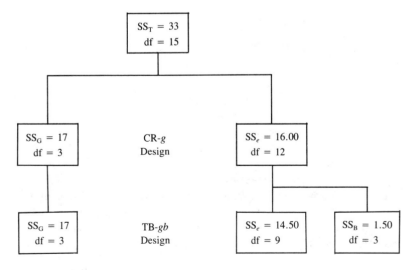

Figure 7.1.

The TB design can therefore be seen to involve a trade-off: Will blocking for the nuisance variable account for a sufficiently large amount of the sum of squares to justify the loss of $b - 1$ degrees of freedom from the error term? As indicated in the row totals of Table 7.1, there turned out to be very little between-row variability, and so in retrospect the blocking was not worth the loss of 3 df from the error term.

Prior to finally accepting the conclusions of the ANOVA in Table 7.2, it is necessary to consider the *additivity assumption* of the TB design— that is, the assumption that each raw score is an additive combination of the overall mean (μ), plus a specific group effect (G), plus a specific block effect (B), plus error (e), or

$$X = \mu + G + B + e$$

In the event of nonadditivity, the variable represented by the blocks (different interviewers in this instance) interacts with the experimental conditions to produce variability over and above the addition of their simple effects. In the nonadditive case,

$$X = \mu + G + B + G \times B + e$$

where $G \times B$ represents the "interaction" of the Groups and Blocks variables. This term signifies that there is a joint effect of these two variables that goes beyond any individual influence.

In this particular experiment, it is possible that the behaviors of subjects within one of the rows are different from those of subjects in the other rows, in which case the overall data configuration represented by the group means would not match the configuration for the deviant row. Were this the case, it would mean that the blocks are interacting with the experimental groups in conflict with the additivity assumption and thereby inflating the error sum of squares, which in turn would increase the size of the denominator of the F ratio and make it more difficult to detect a difference among the various groups.

Tukey's test for additivity is described in reference to Table 7.3. (For further details, consult Kirk, 1982: 250–253.) The unbracketed scores in the interior of the table are the raw scores from Table 7.1; in the side and bottom margins are the row and column means; the overall or grand mean is GM = 4.75; the d scores along the side and bottom are the deviations of the row (d_r) and column (d_c) means around the grand mean; and the numbers in parentheses are the cross-products of the ds in the respective rows and columns. In row 1 and column 3, for example,

$$d_{rc} = d_r \times d_c = d_1 \times d_3 = 0.25 \times 0.75 = 0.19$$

TABLE 7.3

| Blocks | | | Groups | | | |
	1	2	3	4	Mean	d_r
1	5	3	6	6	5.00	0.25
	(−.31)	(−.19)	(.19)	(.31)		
2	3	6	5	5	4.75	0.00
	(.00)	(.00)	(.00)	(.00)		
3	3	2	6	6	4.25	−0.50
	(.63)	(.38)	(−.38)	(−.63)		
4	3	5	5	7	5.00	0.25
	(−.31)	(−.19)	(.19)	(.31)		
Mean	3.50	4.00	5.50	6.00	4.75 = GM	
d_c	−1.25	−0.75	0.75	1.25		

d_r = Row mean − GM
d_c = Column mean − GM

The sums of squares for nonadditivity is given by

$$SS_{nonadd} = \frac{\left(\sum_r \sum_c d_{rc} X\right)^2}{\left(\sum d_r^2\right)\left(\sum d_c^2\right)} \qquad [7.1]$$

where the numerator instructs us to multiply the ds in parentheses by the raw score in the same cell, to sum this cross-product for the entire matrix, and then to square that sum; and the denominator instructs us to multiply the sum of squared row ds by the sum of squared column ds:

$$SS_{nonadd} = \frac{[(-.31)(5) + \cdots + (.31)(7)]^2}{(0.25^2 + \cdots + 0.25^2)(-1.25^2 + \cdots + 1.25^2)}$$

$$= \frac{(-1.25)^2}{(4.25)(0.38)} = 0.98$$

SS_{nonadd} and 1 df are taken from the error term in Table 7.2, leaving a sum of squares for a remainder:

$$SS_{rem} = SS_e - SS_{nonadd} = 14.50 - 0.98 = 13.52$$

$$df_{rem} = df_e - df_{nonadd} = 9 - 1 = 8$$

The F ratio to determine whether the nonadditivity is significant is obtained by forming the ratio of MS_{nonadd} to MS_{rem}:

$$MS_{nonadd} = SS_{nonadd}/df_{nonadd} = 0.98/1 = 0.98$$

$$MS_{rem} = SS_{rem}/df_{rem} = 13.52/8 = 1.69$$

$$F_{nonadd} = 0.98/1.69 = 0.58$$

The F table is consulted for 1 and 8 df, usually at the $\alpha = .25$ level, which, in this case, is $F_{.25; 1, 8} = 1.54$, indicating no significant group $\times$ block interaction, hence the tenability of the additivity assumption. By reducing the alpha level to .25, the experimentalist amplifies sensitivity for the slightest indication of an interaction, at the less serious risk of detecting one where none really exists (Type II error).

If a significant F had been obtained in this example, this would have been an indication that the *sphericity* (or circularity) assumption of randomized block designs had not been met. This assumption concerns a property of the difference scores that can be obtained by subtracting group 2 scores from group 3 scores (for example) for all blocks of subjects. The requirement is that the standard deviations of all possible sets of such difference scores be equivalent (or homogeneous). When this assumption is violated, alternative F tests, adjusted dfs, or data transformations are required. A concise but cogent introduction to this topic is found in Howell (1987).

It is to be noted that the analysis above (see Table 7.1) is based on a situation in which there is only one observation in each group $\times$ block cell, and further that the ANOVA situation would have been different if there had been $n > 1$ observations per cell—for example, with respect to Table 7.1, if rows 1 and 2 contained subjects who had been interviewed by interviewer A and rows 3 and 4 by interviewer B. In that case there would have been $n = 2$ observations per group $\times$ block cell, which would have given rise to the following sources of variance and degrees of freedom:

Groups	$g - 1$	$= 3$
Blocks	$b - 1$	$= 1$
$G \times B$	$(g - 1)(b - 1)$	$= 3$
Error	$gb(n - 1)$	$= 8$
Total	$gnb - 1$	$= 15$

Inasmuch as a design of this kind would be analyzed in precisely the same way (although interpreted somewhat differently) as a completely randomized factorial design with two main effects, the analysis will be postponed to Chapter 9. It should be pointed out, however, that in the TB design when $n > 1$, the interaction between blocks and groups emerges as a separate source of variability, and that there is consequently no need to test for nonadditivity—that is, group $\times$ block interaction is a specified part of the design.

It is also to be noted that the structure of the TB-gb design, in controlling for a single nuisance variable, can be extended to the control of two (Latin square design) or three (Graeco-Latin square design) nuisance variables. These designs are infrequently used, however, and the interested reader is therefore directed to their treatment in any of the more comprehensive texts noted in the References.

In summary, the purpose of the TB-gb design is to control for a potentially contaminating variable or variables (such as interviewer effect in the illustrative case above) which, if left uncontrolled, might inflate the error term and prevent a significant F. Blocking also detracts from the error degrees of freedom, however, and is worthwhile only if the block sum of squares (and/or the interaction sum of squares if $n > 1$) is large enough to offset the loss in error df.

8. ALGORITHMS

To this point, the designs and analyses have been sufficiently straightforward to permit avoidance of complicated subscripts and other notational devices. Similarly, the simplicity of previous designs has rendered the error term (the denominator of the F ratio) fairly obvious: usually it was simply a residual, that is, it was based on the sum of squares remaining after the major effects and their interactions had been accounted for. With the introduction of more complicated designs, however, a more formal notational system becomes advantageous. As will be shown, standardized notation plus a few simple rules will make it possible to employ fairly complicated designs with comparative ease.

8.1. Nesting and Cross-Classifying Subjects

Table 8.1(a) is a completely randomized design and contains the same familiar data as were analyzed in Chapter 5. In this case there is one main

TABLE 8.1

(B)				
B1	B2	B3	B4	
5	3	6	6	
3	6	5	5	
3	2	6	6	
3	5	5	7	
14	16	22	24	76

(a) Completely randomized: $S(B)$

(A)		(B)				
		B1	B2	B3	B4	
	A1	5	3	6	6	39
		3	6	5	5	
	A2	3	2	6	6	37
		3	5	5	7	
		14	16	22	24	76

(b) Completely randomized factorial: $S(AB)$

(A)		(B)							
		B1		B2		B3		B4	
	A1	5	→	3	→	6	→	6	20
		3	→	6	→	5	→	5	19
	A2	3	→	2	→	6	→	6	17
		3	→	5	→	5	→	7	20
		14		16		22		24	76

(c) Split-plot factorial (mixed): $S(A)B$

effect (B) with four levels ($B1$ through $B4$) and $n = 4$ subjects per group, with the group and grand sums as shown at the bottom of the table. The completely randomized factorial in Table 8.1(b) will be discussed in Chapter 9. It is not really a separate design; rather, as shown here, it is a cross-classification of two completely randomized designs: there are two main effects (variable A with two levels, and B with four levels) with $n = 2$ subjects per cell. The split-plot factorial in Table 8.1(c) will be discussed in greater detail in Chapter 10. It is typically referred to as a mixed design because it is the combination of a completely randomized design (variable A) and a repeated measures design (variable B), the latter design being one in which more than one measure is obtained from each subject. In the present instance, the four scores were obtained from each participant, one for each level of B. Hence, the 16 scores in the completely randomized factorial are produced by 16 separate subjects, whereas the same number of scores in the mixed design are produced by only 4 subjects ($n = 2$ in group $A1$, $n = 2$ in group $A2$), each of whom is measured four separate times (i.e., measured for $B1$, $B2$, $B3$, and $B4$).

Because the subjects in the completely randomized factorial design are *nested*, two by two, in each of the eight $A \times B$ cells, this design will be referred to as $S(AB)$, indicating that subjects are nested within the AB cells. [The CR design in Chapter 5 is therefore of the type $S(A)$.] In the mixed design, subjects are randomly assigned to either group $A1$ or to group $A2$, so the A variable distinguishes *between* subjects, and subjects are therefore nested within the A cells. Subjects are exposed to all four levels of variable B, however, hence B is a *within* subjects variable, and subjects are cross-classified with B rather than nested. A shorthand reference for this design will be $S(A)B$, indicating that subjects are nested within the A groups but cross-classified with B.

This design notation supersedes that used in earlier chapters, and its advantage is that it is less generic and provides a more readily accessible description of how the experiment is designed, that is, how subjects have been assigned to experimental treatments. The advantage of the previous notation is that it specifies the number of groups—for example, CR-4 specifies a completely randomized design with $g = 4$ groups—but this can be overcome under the new notation, if need be, through the use of subscripts: hence $S_{10}(A_2 B_4) C_5$ specifies a mixed design with two between-subject variables, A and B, with $a = 2$ and $b = 4$ levels in factorial arrangement; and one within-subjects (repeated measures) variable, C, with $c = 5$ levels; and with $n = 10$ subjects in each of the eight $A \times B$ cells.

8.2. Degrees of Freedom and Sums of Squares

Table 8.2 contains the degrees of freedom for the sources of variance (SV), or variance components, of the $S(AB)$ design in Table 8.1(b). In general, df formulas such as these are obtained by the following heuristic. Let a equal the number of levels of variable A, b equal the number of levels of variable B, etc. Then, for each SV in the ANOVA, let the num-

TABLE 8.2

SV	df Formulas	df	df Formulas Expanded	SS
A	$a - 1$	$= 1 =$	$a - 1$	$SS_A = ASS - CF$
B	$b - 1$	$= 3 =$	$b - 1$	$SS_B = BSS - CF$
AB	$(a - 1)(b - 1)$	$= 3 =$	$ab - a - b + 1$	$SS_{AB} = ABSS - ASS$ $- BSS + CF$
$S(AB)$	$ab(n - 1)$	$= 8 =$	$abn - ab$	$SS_{S(AB)} = TSS - ABSS$
Total	$abn - 1$	$= 15 =$	$abn - 1$	$SS_T = TSS - CF$

ber of levels minus 1 represent the df (e.g., $b - 1$). When the SV is a compound, such as AB, the df are multiplied—for example, $(a - 1)$ $(b - 1)$. For expressions such as $S(AB)$, in which nesting is indicated, the terms in parentheses do not have 1 subtracted from them; thus $S(AB)$ has df $= ab(n - 1)$, where there are n "levels" of subjects.

Moreover, and of greater importance, the df formulas are analogous to a DNA molecule or a Rosetta Stone which, when decoded, provide instructions concerning how to form the required sum of squares for each of the sources of variance. This is begun by expanding the df as shown in Table 8.2—that is, where necessary, carrying through the multiplication indicated. In the case of the $A \times B$ interaction, for example, df $= (a - 1)(b - 1) = ab - a - b + 1$. A list is then made of all the unique symbols and symbol combinations among the expanded df: In this case there are five—1, a, b, ab, and abn—and each represents a component necessary for calculating the sums of squares, both corrected and uncorrected for the mean.

The symbol 1 in all designs represents the correction factor (CF), which is always calculated by summing all scores, squaring that sum, and dividing by the total N. In the $S(AB)$ design of Table 8.1(b), there are $a = 2$ levels of variable A, $b = 4$ levels of B, and $n = 2$ subjects per cell—hence $N = abn = (2)(4)(2) = 16$. The meaning of the symbol 1 is therefore as follows, using the data in Table 8.1(b):

$$1 = CF = \frac{\left(\sum_a \sum_b \sum_n X\right)^2}{abn}$$

$$= \frac{1}{abn}\left(\sum_a \sum_b \sum_n X\right)^2 \tag{8.1}$$

$$= \tfrac{1}{16}(5 + 3 + \cdots + 6 + 7)^2 = 361$$

In this case, the summation signs ($\Sigma_a \Sigma_b \Sigma_n$) indicate that, prior to squaring, the X scores (evaluations of Carter's liberalism) are being summed across all a levels of variable A, all b levels of B, and all n subjects within each cell.

The symbol a represents the uncorrected sum of squares for variable A (ASS), and is decoded as follows:

$$a = \text{ASS} = \sum_a \frac{\left(\sum_b \sum_n X \right)^2}{bn} \qquad [8.2]$$

$$= \frac{1}{bn} \sum_a \left(\sum_b \sum_n X \right)^2$$

The rules for decoding a in expression 8.2, and applicable to all other letter symbols, are:

1. For the letter or letters under consideration (a in this case), enter summation signs, hence Σ_a in expression 8.2.
2. For all other letters not included in the symbol under consideration (b and n in this instance), place summation signs within parentheses, add the symbol for the dependent variable (X), and indicate that the sum is to be squared—hence, $(\Sigma_b \Sigma_n X)^2$ in expression 8.2.
3. Divide the squared sum by the number of observations that comprised the sum—that is, divide by the product of the symbols associated with the summation signs within parentheses. In expression 8.2, the summation signs within parentheses are associated with b and n, hence bn is the divisor.

All that then remains is to interpret the computational formula produced by the application of these rules. In expression 8.2, $\Sigma_a (\Sigma_b \Sigma_n X)^2$ instructs us to form a sum of squares around the differences in the levels of the A variable, that is, around the sums of $A1$ and $A2$ in Table 8.1(b). Specifically, it instructs us (1) to begin with level $A1$ and to sum across all $b = 4$ levels of B and all $n = 2$ subjects per cell, and then (2) to move to level $A2$ and do the same. Each of the sums is then squared, the squared sums are then themselves summed, and the total is divided by bn, or, alternatively, multiplied by $1/(bn)$. The operations using the data in Table 8.1(b) and expression 8.2 are as follows:

$$a = \text{ASS} = \tfrac{1}{8}[(5 + 3 + \cdots + 6 + 5)^2$$
$$+ (3 + 3 + \cdots + 6 + 7)^2]$$
$$= \tfrac{1}{8}(39^2 + 37^2) = 361.25$$

By the same token, the symbol b designates the uncorrected sum of squares for the B variable (BSS)—that is, in terms of the data in Table 8.1(b), the column totals are to be squared and added together, and then divided by $1/(an)$. Applying the decoding rules:

$$b = \text{BSS} = \frac{1}{an} \sum_b \left(\sum_a \sum_n X \right)^2$$
$$= \tfrac{1}{4}(14^2 + 16^2 + 22^2 + 24^2) = 378 \qquad [8.3]$$

ab symbolizes the uncorrected sum of squares for the interaction of variables A and B (indicated by ABSS), and directs comparison of the $ab = 8$ cells in Table 8.1(b):

$$ab = \text{ABSS} = \frac{1}{n} \sum_a \sum_b \left(\sum_n X \right)^2$$
$$= \tfrac{1}{2}[(5 + 3)^2 + \cdots + (6 + 7)^2] \qquad [8.4]$$
$$= \tfrac{1}{2}(8^2 + 9^2 + \cdots + 11^2 + 13^2) = 381$$

Finally, abn includes all three of the letter symbols in this design, and hence stands for the uncorrected total sum of squares (TSS). Because all letters are included, there are no letters in parentheses and no divisor. The decoding rules applied yield:

$$abn = \text{TSS} = \sum_a \sum_b \sum_n X^2$$
$$= 5^2 + 3^2 + \cdots + 6^2 + 7^2 = 394 \qquad [8.5]$$

The degrees of freedom, once decoded, not only give directions about how to calculate the uncorrected sums of squares and the correction factor, but, as shown in Table 8.2, also indicate how to combine these figures to produce the corrected sums of squares. In the case of variable A, for example, $df_A = a - 1$, hence the corrected sum of squares for this variable is given by $SS_A = \text{ASS} - \text{CF} = 361.25 - 361 = 0.25$. In the case of the AB interaction, $df_{AB} = (a - 1)(b - 1) = ab - a - b + 1$; the corrected sum of squares is therefore $SS_{AB} = \text{ABSS} - \text{ASS} - \text{BSS} + \text{CF} = 381 - 361.25 - 378 + 361 = 2.75$.

The mean squares are then calculated as in previous sections (i.e., $\text{MS} = \text{SS}/\text{df}$), and the F ratio is formed by dividing the MS for each variance component (A, B, and AB) by the error MS. According to the new notation, the error MS for this design is designated $\text{MS}_{S(AB)}$ because $S(AB)$ refers to subjects within a cell, and hence designates the experi-

TABLE 8.3

SV	Degrees of Freedom		SS
	Formulas	Expanded	
Between Subjects	$an - 1$	$= an - 1$	$SS_{BS} = ANSS - CF$
A	$a - 1$	$= a - 1$	$SS_A = ASS - CF$
$S(A)$	$a(n - 1)$	$= an - a$	$SS_{S(A)} = ANSS - ASS$
Within Subjects	$an(b - 1)$	$= abn - an$	$SS_{WS} = TSS - ANSS$
B	$b - 1$	$= b - 1$	$SS_B = BSS - CF$
AB	$(a - 1)(b - 1)$	$= ab - a - b + 1$	$SS_{AB} = ABSS - ASS$ $- BSS + CF$
$S(A)B$	$a(b - 1)(n - 1)$	$= abn - ab - an + a$	$SS_{S(A)B} = TSS$ $- ABSS$ $- ANSS$ $+ ASS$
Total	$abn - 1$	$= abn - 1$	$SS_T = TSS - CF$

mental space in which subjects are treated identically. Because subjects were assigned to cells on a random basis, their differences in score must therefore be due to random influences.

The same computational logic can be extended to the mixed, or $S(A)B$, design in Table 8.1(c). The expanded degrees of freedom for this design are displayed in Table 8.3. In this case, there are six unique symbols and symbol combinations contained in the expanded df, hence six computations to perform: 1, a, an, b, ab, and abn. The symbol an is the only one not contained in the previous example, and in relation to the figures in Table 8.1(c) produces the following:

$$an = ANSS = \frac{1}{b} \sum_a \sum_n \left(\sum_b X \right)^2 \qquad [8.6]$$
$$= \tfrac{1}{4}\left[(5 + 3 + 6 + 6)^2 + \cdots + (3 + 5 + 5 + 7)^2 \right]$$
$$= \tfrac{1}{4}(20^2 + 19^2 + 17^2 + 20^2) = 362.5$$

Hence, ANSS measures the degree of differences among the rows (i.e., overall differences among the subjects) in Table 8.1(c). The corrected sums of squares are obtained by combining the calculations as dictated by the expanded df, as shown in the SS column in Table 8.3.

The decoding rules above can be applied to the completely randomized design and to all designs considered in subsequent chapters, which encompasses a large proportion of the designs in general use in the social and psychological sciences. Given a particular design, therefore, all that is required is to know the general formulas for the degrees of freedom for the variance components. Given the df formulas, it is a simple matter to expand them, to construct the computational formulas to which they lead, and to combine the calculations to provide the corrected sums of squares, which, in turn, lead to the mean squares and F ratios.

8.3. Mean Squares and F Ratios

Without going into unnecessary statistical detail, it is important to appreciate that when two or more columns of numbers are separately summed, more than just a group effect is captured. Consider the $S(AB)$ design of Table 8.1(b): When comparing row differences (A), column differences (B), or cell differences (AB), the sums of squares involved necessarily include within-cell variability (error), for which $SS_{S(AB)}$ (in Table 8.2) provides an independent measure. The F ratio for testing variable A is therefore

$$F = \frac{MS_A}{MS_{S(AB)}}$$

$$= \frac{\text{between levels of } A}{\text{error}}$$

$$= \frac{\text{error} + A}{\text{error}} = 1 + \frac{A}{\text{error}}$$

Hence, the F ratio equals 1.00 plus some amount reflecting the extent to which the A effect exceeds within-cell error. If, as under H_0, the levels of A do not differ, then $F = 1.00 + 0.00$. The F ratio will always have an expected value greater than 1.00 when the alternative hypothesis (H_1) is true, and an expected value of approximately 1.00 when H_0 is true.

In general, a *valid F ratio* is one in which the denominator contains all the components that are in the numerator except for the component that is being tested. If the numerator contains error plus A, and if A is the component to be tested, then the denominator must contain error. If the numerator is $A + B + C$ and the effect to be tested is B, then the denominator must be $A + C$. With more complicated designs, simplified rules are needed to designate those F ratios that will provide appropriate tests of the significance of effects of interest.

Focusing on the $S(AB)$ design in Table 8.1(b) and its source of vari-

TABLE 8.4

	Mean Square Components				
SV	S(AB)	AB	B	A	F ratio
1 A	*			*	$\frac{1}{4}$
2 B	*		*		$\frac{2}{4}$
3 AB	*	*			$\frac{3}{4}$
4 S(AB)	*				—

(a) S(AB) fixed effects model

	S(A'B')	A'B'	B'	A'	
1 A'	*	*		*	$\frac{1}{3}$
2 B'	*	*	*		$\frac{2}{3}$
3 A'B'	*	*			$\frac{3}{4}$
4 S(A'B')	*				—

(b) S(A'B') random effects model

	S(A'B)	A'B	B	A'	
1 A'	*			*	$\frac{1}{4}$
2 B	*	*	*		$\frac{2}{3}$
3 A'B	*	*			$\frac{3}{4}$
4 S(A'B)	*				—

(c) S(A'B) mixed effects model

ance table in Table 8.2, the rules for forming the appropriate F ratio can be given with respect to Table 8.4(a) (modified after Schultz, 1955):

1. List all sources of variance below SV (source of variance)—in this case A, B, AB, and S(AB), which are numbered for convenience—and list them again in reverse order across the top of the table.
2. In each row, place an asterisk in the column associated with the variance component under consideration. (Hence, in row 1, which is associated with component A, an asterisk is placed in column A; in row 2, an asterisk is placed in column B; etc.)
3. In each row, also place an asterisk in each column associated with the variance component under consideration if it appears with other components that are not within parentheses and that are random variables.

Rule 3 refers to a distinction to be made below between fixed and random variables. For the moment, suffice it to say for the S(AB) design that variable B is not random: A appears with B in the interaction term, AB, and B is not enclosed within parentheses, so an asterisk would appear in column AB of row 1 if B were random; but B is not random, so that column remains blank. The B column remains blank for row 1 because A does not appear in it. Experimental subjects are always a random effect, hence an asterisk appears in column $S(AB)$ of row 1—that is, A appears in $S(AB)$, S is outside parentheses, and S is a random variable, and this qualifies for an asterisk under rule 3. Rows 2, 3, and 4 are completed in the same fashion.

A valid F ratio, as stated previously, is one in which the denominator contains all the components that are in the numerator except for the component that is being tested. As indicated in the F column of Table 8.4(a), the ratio for testing the A variable is the mean square for component 1 divided by the mean square for component 4:

$$F = \frac{\mathrm{MS}_A}{\mathrm{MS}_{S(AB)}}$$
$$= \frac{S(AB) + A}{S(AB)}$$

The numerator contains the two components designated by asterisks in row 1, and the denominator contains the one component designated by an asterisk in row 4. The ratio of mean square components therefore satisfies the criterion for a valid F test, and the same procedures are followed to test the significance of B and AB. It should be mentioned that, in the statistical literature, the mean square components in Table 8.4 are typically referred to as *expected mean squares*.

In the $S(A)$ design of Chapter 5, it was assumed that interest focused on the four experimental groups under consideration—that is, group 1 (Carter with three liberals), group 2 (Carter with two liberals and one conservative), and so forth. This is referred to as a *fixed effects model* because interest is in these four groups and no others. However, had the four groups been regarded as simply four representatives drawn at random from a larger population of groups, then the Groups variable would have been a random rather than a fixed variable, hence a *random effects model*. In the latter model, any conclusions reached concerning a statistically significant Groups effect would need to encompass the entire population of treatment conditions from which the four in the experiment were sampled. In a fixed effects model, conclusions would be limited to the actual treatment conditions employed. In the case of the $S(A)$ design, the distinction is of no consequence insofar as the F ratio is concerned because the testing procedure is the same regardless of whether variable A is fixed or random.

In other designs, however, the fixed or random status of variables does influence which mean squares enter into a valid F ratio, and for the sake of clarity a prime sign (') will henceforth designate variables that are random (with the aforementioned exception of the subjects variable, designated S, which is always random). Variable A is fixed, therefore, whereas A' is random, and AB' specifies an interaction between fixed variable A and random variable B', $S(A'B')$ denotes that subjects are nested in two-variable cells in a design in which both main effects are random variables.

Returning to Table 8.1(b), assume that both main effects are random, that is, that the design is of the type $S(A'B')$. Table 8.4(b) indicates the mean square components and the appropriate F ratios using Schultz's rules above. In this instance, the denominator to test the A' effect would be the $A'B'$ interaction. If A' was random and B fixed, as in Table 8.4(c), the denominator to test A' would be the mean square for within cells, $S(A'B)$. Hence, what qualifies as experimental error and what does not depends on the nature of the design.

To indicate how Schultz's rules operate in the mixed design, assume that the variables in Table 8.1(c) are both fixed, as in Table 8.5(a). In this case, the MS for A is tested against the MS for $S(A)$, whereas the within-subjects components are tested against the MS for $S(A)B$.

With variable B' random, as in Table 8.5(b), the formation of each F ratio is straightforward except in the case of variable A, which requires what is termed a "quasi-F" because of the fact that there is no single mean square with the appropriate characteristics necessary for the denominator. A "pooled" mean square is therefore formed using components 2 plus 4 minus 5:

$$\mathrm{MS_{pooled}} = \mathrm{MS}_{S(A)} + \mathrm{MS}_{AB'} - \mathrm{MS}_{S(A)B'}$$
$$= [S(A)B' + S(A)] + [S(A)B' + AB'] - S(A)B'$$
$$= S(A)B' + AB' + S(A)$$

The F ratio to test variable A is therefore:

$$F = \frac{\mathrm{MS}_A}{\mathrm{MS_{pooled}}}$$
$$= \frac{S(A)B' + AB' + S(A) + A}{S(A)B' + AB' + S(A)}$$

TABLE 8.5

SV	Mean Square Components					F ratio
	$S(A)B$	AB	B	$S(A)$	A	
Bet. Subjects						—
1 A				*	*	$\frac{1}{2}$
2 $S(A)$				*		—
W/in Subjects						—
3 B	*		*			$\frac{3}{5}$
4 AB	*	*				$\frac{4}{5}$
5 $S(A)B$	*					—

(a) $S(A)B$ fixed effects model

	$S(A)B'$	AB'	B'	$S(A)$	A	
Bet. Subjects						—
1 A	*	*		*	*	$1/(2 + 4 - 5)$
2 $S(A)$	*			*		$\frac{2}{5}$
W/in Subjects						—
3 B'	*		*			$\frac{3}{5}$
4 AB'	*	*				$\frac{4}{5}$
5 $S(A)B'$	*					—

(b) $S(A)B'$ mixed effects model

The variance components in the denominator therefore contain all the components that are in the numerator except for that component (variable A in this case) that is being tested, as is required for a valid F. It is to be noted that in order to be exact, this F requires a pooling of degrees of freedom for the denominator, a topic that will be covered in Chapter 10.

The purpose of this notational and algorithmic interlude has been to introduce relatively simple rules that will facilitate the analysis of designs of greater complexity. The design labels, for example, $S(AB)C$, symbolize how the design is structured. The "decoding rules" show how computational formulas for the sums of squares can be constructed, based upon a knowledge of the formulas for degrees of freedom. Once the corrected sums of squares are calculated—and the directions for this are also coded in the degrees of freedom—the mean squares are gotten as usual, $MS = SS/df$. Schultz's rules then designate which mean squares to combine for valid F ratios. These rules apply retrospectively to the completely randomized design, and to all other designs that will be considered subsequently, and to designs of the fixed, random, or mixed-effects varieties.

9. FACTORIAL DESIGN

The factorial design, as mentioned previously, is not really a separate class of design, but a way of combining two or more designs. As a case in point, consider the completely randomized design discussed in Chapter 5: The investigator, recall, wished to examine the impact of political anchors on assessments of President Carter's liberalism (dependent variable), but suppose that another investigator were interested in examining the impact on the same dependent variable of exposure to a conservative critique of the Carter Administration.

The data in Table 9.1 are for another purpose, to be described momentarily, but the design structure is congruent with the problem just described, where $A1$ through $A4$ would be the same as the anchor variable examined in Chapter 5, and the B variable would represent exposure ($B1$) versus no exposure ($B2$) to a conservative critique. There would therefore be $ab = (4)(2) = 8$ cells into which respondents would be assigned. (In this case, there are $n = 5$ subjects per treatment combination.) Although half of the respondents in the $A1$ condition would be exposed to a conservative message and half would not, this would not bias the mean of $A1$ because the respondents in the $A2$, $A3$, and $A4$ conditions would be treated in the same way. The effect of the B variable would therefore be balanced across each of the conditions of A, and so the 40 responses could be conceived as being devoted solely to a test of the A variable; alternatively, the same 40 responses (20 each in $B1$ and $B2$) could be treated as if the A variable did not exist. The Table 9.1 design therefore contains two completely randomized designs which have been arranged factorially, and the greater efficiency that this arrangement provides arises from the fact that each respondent serves a double function.

More typically, a single investigator with interest in both variables will enter them into the same experiment in order to estimate their separate plus interactive effects on the dependent variable. In the case of Table 9.1, interest centered on the effect of reading instruction strategy (variable A) and gender (B) on the percentage increase in reading accuracy (dependent variable based on a word recognition test) of third-grade dyslexic children: $A1$ was a control group (no special instruction), $A2$ received whole word (visual) instruction, $A3$ received phonics instruction, and $A4$ received mulitisensory instruction. Strictly speaking, gender is of course not an experimental variable—rather, it is a subject variable or characteristic—but it will be treated as such for illustrative purposes.

The results of the ANOVA are shown in Table 9.2 (assuming a fixed

TABLE 9.1

| | Learning Strategies | | | | Total | Mean |
	A1	A2	A3	A4		
B1	44	54	60	86		
Male	33	53	47	89		
	55	55	68	86	1250	62.50
	57	57	72	81		
	51	56	75	71		
	(240)[a]	(275)	(322)	(413)		
B2	37	56	54	55		
Female	37	63	37	50		
	30	60	58	44	1017	50.85
	48	61	55	57		
	50	48	61	56		
	(202)	(288)	(265)	(262)		
Total	442	563	587	675	2267	Grand sum
Mean	44.20	56.30	58.70	67.50	56.68	GM
					136,005	TSS

[a]Cell totals are in parentheses.

TABLE 9.2

SV	df			SS	MS	F
Strategy (A)	a − 1	=	3	2770.48	923.49	14.88**
Gender (B)	b − 1	=	1	1357.23	1357.23	21.87**
A × B	(a − 1)(b − 1)	=	3	1409.07	469.69	7.57**
S(AB)	ab(n − 1)	=	32	1986.00	62.06	
Total	abn − 1	=	39	7522.78		

**$p < .01$

effects model) and were obtained by applying the rules discussed in the previous chapter. An expansion of the df, for example, yields five unique symbols and symbol combinations which, when decoded, produce the following computational formulas and uncorrected sums of squares (for $a = 4$ levels of A, $b = 2$ levels of B, and $n = 5$ subjects per cell):

$$1 = CF = \frac{1}{abn}\left(\sum_a \sum_b \sum_n X\right)^2$$
$$= \tfrac{1}{40}(2267)^2 = 128,482.22$$

$$a = \text{ASS} = \frac{1}{bn}\sum_a\left(\sum_b\sum_n X\right)^2$$
$$= \tfrac{1}{10}(442^2 + 563^2 + 587^2 + 675^2) = 131,252.70$$

$$b = \text{BSS} = \frac{1}{an}\sum_b\left(\sum_a\sum_n X\right)^2$$
$$= \tfrac{1}{20}(1250^2 + 1017^2) = 129,839.45$$

$$ab = \text{ABSS} = \frac{1}{n}\sum_a\sum_b\left(\sum_n X\right)^2$$
$$= \tfrac{1}{5}(240^2 + 202^2 + \cdots + 262^2) = 134,019.00$$

$$abn = \text{TSS} = \sum_a\sum_b\sum_n X^2$$
$$= 44^2 + \cdots + 56^2 = 136,005.00$$

The expanded df also specify how to combine the uncorrected sums of squares to produce the corrected sums:

$$SS_A = a - 1 = \text{ASS} - \text{CF} = 131,252.70 - 128,482.22 = 2770.48$$
$$SS_B = b - 1 = \text{BSS} - \text{CF} = 129,839.45 - 128,482.22 = 1357.23$$

$$SS_{AB} = ab - a - b + 1 = \text{ABSS} - \text{ASS} - \text{BSS} + \text{CF}$$
$$= 134,019.00 - 131,252.70 - 129,839.45 + 128,482.22$$
$$= 1409.07$$

$$SS_{S(AB)} = abn - ab = \text{TSS} - \text{ABSS}$$
$$= 136,005.00 - 134,019.00 = 1986.00$$

$$SS_T = abn - 1 = \text{TSS} - \text{CF}$$
$$= 136,005.00 - 128,482.22 = 7522.78$$

The corrected SS, when divided by their respective df, yield the appropriate mean squares in the MS column of Table 9.2. The next task is to determine which MS to employ in forming valid F tests.

Employing Schultz's algorithm, the components of the four mean squares and the appropriate F ratios are as follows:

1. $MS_A = S(AB) + A \qquad F = 1/4 = 923.49/62.06 = 14.88$

2. $MS_B = S(AB) + B$ $\qquad F = 2/4 = 1357.22/62.06 = 21.87$

3. $MS_{AB} = S(AB) + AB$ $\qquad F = 3/4 = 469.69/62.06 = 7.57$

4. $MS_{S(AB)} = S(AB)$

In this case—that is, with both A and B fixed, and with subjects nested within AB cells—the mean square for $S(AB)$ is the appropriate divisor for both main effects and their interaction. The df in Table 9.2 then specify which column and row to enter in the F table (Appendix B). For the A effect, the F table is entered for $df_A = 3$ and $df_{S(AB)} = 32$: $F_{.05;3,32} = 2.90$ (approximately), which is exceeded by the above calculated $F = 14.88$, which is therefore significant ($p < .05$). Indeed, all three Fs above are significant beyond the $\alpha = .01$ level.

Before turning to the a posteriori testing of means, consider the modifications in the F test that would have been required had variable A above been random rather than fixed—that is, had the four learning strategies in Table 9.1 been merely four selected at random from a wider collection of possible strategies. In this hypothetical situation, which is somewhat far-fetched conceptually, the mean squares and F ratios would have been as follows:

1. $MS_{A'} = S(A'B) + A'$

   $F = 1/4 = 923.49/62.06 = 14.88$

2. $MS_B = S(A'B) + A'B + B$

   $F = 2/3 = 1357.22/469.69 = 2.89$

3. $MS_{A'B} = S(A'B) + A'B$

   $F = 3/4 = 469.69/62.06 = 7.57$

4. $MS_{S(A'B)} = S(A'B)$

Whereas variable A' and the $A'B$ interaction remain significant ($p < .01$) as before, the B variable is no longer significant because of the fact that a larger number ($MS_{A'B} = 469.69$ rather than $MS_{S(A'B)} = 62.06$) is now required in the denominator for a valid F test. Whether a design is fixed, random, or mixed, therefore, does not influence the sizes of the mean squares, which are calculated in the same way regardless of the type of design; however, design type does influence which MS is chosen for the denominator, and this can influence the size of F and the conclusions drawn.

9.1. A Posteriori Testing

Table 9.2 indicates that both A and B as well as their interaction are significant, which invites the a posteriori testing of means. The significance of the AB interaction implies that the behavior of the A variable was different in $B1$ compared with $B2$—or, in this instance, that the pattern of means (for improvement in reading accuracy) for the various learning strategies was different for male than for female dyslexics. Although A and B were significant, therefore, caution should be taken in rendering general statements about these effects—for example, about the superior effectiveness of a specific learning strategy or of either of the sexes compared with the other—because the performances of either A or B are conditioned by specific levels of the other.

Table 9.3 contains the four teaching strategy means ($A1$ to $A4$) for males ($B1$) and females ($B2$), with significant mean differences shown in the interior of the tables. Tukey's HSD test, defined in expression 6.5, was employed for a posteriori testing and necessitates the calculation of $q_{HSD} = d/S_{\bar{X}}$, where d stands for any difference under consideration, and the standard error of the mean ($S_{\bar{X}}$) is given by $\sqrt{MS_e/n}$. In this case, there are $n = 5$ subjects in each of the AB cells to be compared, and the error mean square from Table 9.2 is associated with $S(AB)$, that is, the error estimate placed in the denominator of the F ratio when testing for the significance of the AB interaction. In this instance, therefore, $S_{\bar{X}} = \sqrt{62.06/5} = 3.52$.

Applied to the male subjects' means, the most extreme means yield a difference of $d = 82.60 - 48.00 = 34.60$, and the test value is consequently $q_{HSD} = 34.60/3.52 = 9.83$, which easily exceeds the critical Studentized range value of 4.80 for a range of $r = 4$ means, $\alpha = .01$, and $df_e = 32$ from Table 9.2 (see Appendix D). Asterisks in Table 9.3 indicate the other significant differences determined in the same fashion.

The interpretation of the data in Table 9.3 demonstrates the conditional nature of conclusions concerning main effects when their interaction is significant. Whereas the patterns of the means show that the no-treatment control group ($A1$) performed generally less well for both males and females, they also show that the difference for males between control and visual strategy ($A2$) was not significant. Although each of the teaching strategies was better than no treatment for the females, none of the strategies was demonstrably better than any other; for the males, however, the multisensory strategy ($A4$) proved superior to any of the others.

The standard error of the mean above ($S_{\bar{X}} = 3.52$) can also be used to

TABLE 9.3

		Group Means (males)		
	A4	A3	A2	A1
	82.60	64.40	55.00	48.00
A4 82.60	—	18.20**	27.60**	34.60**
A3 64.40		—	9.40	16.40**
A2 55.00			—	7.00
A1 48.00	$S_{\bar{X}} = 3.52$			—

		Group Means (females)		
	A2	A3	A4	A1
	57.60	53.00	52.40	40.40
A2 57.60	—	4.60	5.20	17.20**
A3 53.00		—	0.60	12.60*
A4 52.40			—	12.00*
A1 40.40	$S_{\bar{X}} = 3.52$			—

*$p < .05$, **$p < .01$

test the differences between gender means for each of the levels of variable A. When this is done, only two emerge as significant—at $A3$ ($p < .05$) and $A4$ ($p < .01$).

The issue of multiple comparisons for interactions is somewhat contentious. It is sometimes suggested that all cells be considered as in an $S(A)$ design: In the example in Table 9.1, this would lead to the use of Tukey's test with $r = 8$, but this strategy often leads to comparisons that are confounded, for example, $A1$ females versus $A4$ males. Perhaps the most reasonable alternative is that offered by Keppel (1973: 244-246), where α_{fw} is divided over the number of rows or columns to be analyzed. In the example above, there are four columns or two rows to be examined; thus an alpha of $.05/2$ or $.05/4$ would be used in each analysis (or $.05/6$ were the interaction to be examined in terms of rows and also columns). The difficulty of course is that there are no tables for the $q = .05/2 = .025$ level, such as would be necessary for the present analysis of rows. The simplest solution is to adopt a $.01$ alpha level: This would lead to a loss of power and a consequent increase in Type II errors, but it is recommended given the prevailing view in applied statistics concerning the need to control Type I errors in post hoc analyses. A thorough discussion of simple effects analysis and interaction comparisons is in Keppel (1982: 208–245).

9.2. Hierarchical Designs

Hierarchical designs often bear resemblance to completely randomized factorial designs: they differ inasmuch as they involve multiple nesting, that is, complete cross-classification is lacking. In the factorial design considered previously (see Table 9.1), each level of B appears with each level of A so that the interaction of the two can be determined; however, the situation in Table 9.4 is different.

In this case, variable A represents two different teaching strategies (visual and verbal). The scores are the same as in Table 9.1, but the situation has been restructured to picture an experiment consisting of four teachers of dyslexic students, to each of whom $n = 10$ cases are randomly assigned. (For this design, ignore the gender variable C.) Although there are $b = 2$ teachers for each level of A, the two assigned to level $A1$ are different from the two under level $A2$; hence, teachers are nested under teaching strategy, that is, $B(A)$, and it is therefore impossible to determine any AB interaction.

Similarly, subjects are nested within the B variable, that is, $S[B(A)]$; hence it cannot be known whether students nested under teacher $B1$ would have performed in the same way if nested instead under teacher $B2$. The nested effect is random in this instance because it is assumed that the four teachers were randomly chosen from a population of such individuals.

TABLE 9.4

	Teaching Strategy (A)			
	(A1) Visual		(A2) Verbal	
	Teachers (B)			
	B1	B2	B3	B4	
Male	44	54	60	86	
(C1)	33	53	47	89	
	55	55	68	86	
	57	57	72	81	
	51	56	75	71	
Female	37	56	54	55	
(C2)	37	63	37	50	
	30	60	58	44	
	48	61	55	57	
	50	48	61	56	
	442	563	587	675	2267

Most often, nested variables are random; consequently, as in the case of the subjects variable S, the prime sign would be redundant and will therefore be omitted in the following analysis.

The ANOVA results are shown in Table 9.5, where $a = 2$ teaching strategies, $b = 2$ teachers nested within each A, and $n = 10$ subjects nested within B. (Note that there are $b = 2$ teachers per level of A although the two in $A1$ are different from those in $A2$.) The four computations for uncorrected sums of squares, based on the symbols in the expanded df, are:

$$1 = CF = \tfrac{1}{40}(2267)^2 = 128,482.22$$

$$a = ASS = \tfrac{1}{20}\big[(442 + 563)^2 + (587 + 675)^2\big] = 130,133.45$$

$$ab = ABSS = \tfrac{1}{10}(442^2 + \cdots + 675^2) = 131,252.70$$

$$abn = TSS = 44^2 + 33^2 + \cdots + 57^2 + 56^2 = 136,005.00$$

The corrected sums of squares, mean squares, and F ratios are displayed in Table 9.5, and the following expected mean square components, based on Schultz's rules, indicate what ratios had to be formed for valid F tests:

1. A $S[B(A)] + B(A) + A$ $F = 1/2$

2. $B(A)$ $S[B(A)] + B(A)$ $F = 2/3$

3. $S[B(A)]$ $S[B(A)]$

According to Schultz's rules, the appropriate ratio for testing variable A is $F = MS_A/MS_{B(A)}$, which is not significant. The test for the B variable ($F = MS_{B(A)}/MS_{S[B(A)]}$) is significant, however, and would be interpreted as demonstrating that some teachers were more effective than others in producing improvements in reading accuracy, regardless of teaching strategy. Ordinarily, the B variable is not of interest because, as in this

TABLE 9.5

SV	df			SS	MS	F
1 A	$a - 1$	$= 1$	$= a - 1$	1651.23	1651.23	2.95
2 $B(A)$	$a(b - 1)$	$= 2$	$= ab - a$	1119.25	559.62	4.24*
3 $S[B(A)]$	$ab(n - 1)$	$= 36$	$= abn - ab$	4752.30	132.01	
Total	$abn - 1$	$= 39$	$= abn - 1$	7522.78		

*$p < .05$

instance, the four randomly selected teachers were not intrinsic to the experiment except in the procedural sense of facilitating its execution.

As shown here, variable A is frequently insignificant because the df associated with the denominator of the F test is normally quite small ($df_{B(A)} = 2$ this example). It is always possible, therefore, that A might prove significant were a more sensitive test available. In the usual case in which $B(A)$ is not significant, this source of variance can be pooled with $S[B(A)]$ for a more powerful error MS. This pooling is inadmissible, however, if there is the slightest chance that $B(A)$ is significant, and so this source of variance is usually tested at a very low level (e.g., $\alpha = .25$). In the above case, as indicated, $B(A)$ is highly significant, and so pooling would be strictly inadmissible. For the sake of illustrating procedure, however, this will be ignored and the pooling will proceed by combining the sums of squares for $B(A)$ and $S[B(A)]$ and dividing by their combined df:

$$MS_{pooled} = \frac{SS_{B(A)} + SS_{S[B(A)]}}{df_{B(A)} + df_{S[B(A)]}}$$

$$= \frac{1119.25 + 4752.30}{2 + 36} = 154.51$$

The revised F ratio, based on the pooling above and the analysis in Table 9.5, is now

$$F = MS_A/MS_{pooled} = 1651.23/154.51 = 10.69 \quad (p < .01)$$

with 1 and 38 df associated with the numerator and denominator, respectively. Had the pooling been admissible, the result would have indicated a significant difference between teaching strategies $A1$ and $A2$.

Hierarchical designs can also contain variables that are arranged factorially, and this can be demonstrated by returning to Table 9.4 and taking into account the gender variable C. As previously, B is nested within A, but C is cross-classified with both A and B, which gives rise to the sources of variance in Table 9.6.

The calculations leading to the ANOVA in Table 9.6 are left as an exercise. Interpretation of the results would give special emphasis to the significant $B(A)C$ interaction, which indicates that male and female students (variable C) performed differently depending on the teacher to which they were assigned (variable B). It would be the task of a posteriori testing to tease out the salient differences that were contributing to this significant F.

TABLE 9.6

SV	df			SS	MS		F
Between							
Levels of A							
1 A	$a - 1$	=	1	1651.23	1651.23	$\frac{1}{2}$	2.95
2 $B(A)$	$a(b - 1)$	=	2	1119.25	559.63	$\frac{2}{6}$	9.02**
Within							
Levels of A							
3 C	$c - 1$	=	1	1357.23	1357.23	$\frac{3}{5}$	4.75
4 AC	$(a - 1)(c - 1)$	=	1	837.23	837.23	$\frac{4}{5}$	2.93
5 $B(A)C$	$a(b - 1)(c - 1)$	=	2	571.85	285.93	$\frac{5}{6}$	4.61*
Subjects							
Within Cells							
6 $S[B(A)C]$	$abc(n - 1)$	=	32	1986.00	62.06		
Total	$abcn - 1$	=	39	7522.78			

*$p < .05$; **$p < .01$

Factorial designs are probably the most widely used in the social sciences because of their simplicity as well as the fact that they permit the simultaneous examination of two or more main effects plus their interactions. A major advantage is their efficiency because each subject is, in effect, used in two or more experiments—that is, each subject's dependent score (e.g., reading improvement) is used as part of the design evaluating variable A and again for evaluating B (and C, D, etc.). Hierarchical designs are useful when it is not convenient completely to cross-classify the variables of interest. Nested effects are generally of little interest, but (as in the case of the teachers in Table 9.4) are necessary to expedite the experiment. The impact of their presence in the experiment must therefore be evaluated.

10. SPLIT-PLOT AND REPEATED MEASURES DESIGNS

The split-plot and repeated measures designs differ from others previously covered by virtue of the fact that subjects are measured more than once on the dependent variable—hence the term "repeated measures," a design that has been somewhat controversial (Lovie, 1981). The split-plot terminology derives from agriculture, where plots of ground were divided, each subplot then receiving a different experimental treatment. Within the human sciences, the term *mixed design* has been increasingly adopted to refer to those experiments in which there are both within-subjects (repeated measures) and between-subjects variables. Another way of viewing the designs described in this chapter is to regard them as a subset of the treatments × blocks designs of Chapter 7, with individual subjects being analogous to blocks in the TB design.

Consider Table 10.1 as an example. In this study, subjects were instructed to respond to a set of possible public policies (e.g., reducing taxes, increasing social security benefits), first in terms of the extent to which they saw these policies as benefitting or costing them personally (along a 2 to −2 benefit/cost continuum), and second in terms of the extent to which they thought the current Republican Administration supported or opposed the same policies (assessed along the same 2 to −2 continuum). The policies reflected a range of values, including *wealth* (*W*), for example, protecting banks and businesses from failure; *well-being* (*B*), increasing the availability of low-cost medical treatment; *respect* (*R*), equalizing opportunities for women and minorities; and *rectitude* (*D*), legalizing prayer in the public schools. The resulting difference scores reflected the extent to which subjects judged their value preferences to be in accord with the Republican Administration's policy initiatives—positive scores indicating congruence, negative scores incongruence. Each subject therefore provided four scores, one for each of the four values.

It will be recalled that in the completely randomized design considered in Chapter 5, there were 16 subjects (each of whom was measured only once), with $n = 4$ being nested within each group; this was referred to as an $S(A)$ design, indicating that subjects were nested within each level of

TABLE 10.1

| Subjects | Values (A) | | | | | |
	W	B	R	D	Sum	
S1	1	4	0	−1	4	
S2	2	−8	2	1	−3	
S3	2	−7	1	2	−2	
S4	0	−5	−7	1	−11	
S5	−2	−8	0	−4	−14	
Sum	3	−24	−4	−1	−26	Grand sum
Mean	0.60	−4.80	−0.80	−0.20	−1.30	GM
					308	TSS

A. By way of contrast, the repeated measure design in Table 10.1 is of the type SA, with subjects being cross-classified with each level of A. In the $S(A)$ design, the error MS contains all uncontrolled sources of variance, including variability arising from individual differences among subjects. One of the advantages of the SA design, therefore, is that it provides an assessment of the amount of total sum of squares attributable to differences among subjects, which is then subtracted from the error term, thereby reducing the size of the denominator of the F ratio.

The ANOVA of the data in Table 10.1 is summarized in Table 10.2. As illustrated previously, the expanded df can be used to determine the corrected SS, following the decoding rules of Chapter 8. In this case, there are four symbols and symbol combinations:

$$1 = CF = \frac{1}{an}\left(\sum_a \sum_n X\right)^2$$
$$= \tfrac{1}{20}(-26)^2 = 33.80$$

$$n = SSS = \frac{1}{a}\sum_n\left(\sum_a X\right)^2$$
$$= \tfrac{1}{4}\left[(4)^2 + \cdots + (-14)^2\right] = 86.50$$

$$a = ASS = \frac{1}{n}\sum_a\left(\sum_n X\right)^2$$
$$= \tfrac{1}{5}\left[(3)^2 + \cdots + (-1)^2\right] = 120.40$$

$$an = TSS = \sum_a \sum_n X^2$$
$$= 1^2 + 2^2 + \cdots + 1^2 + (-4)^2 = 308.00$$

where SSS is the uncorrected sum of squares arising from differences among subjects. The expanded df for the SA term is $(a - 1)(n - 1) =$

TABLE 10.2

SV	df		SS	MS	F
Among subjects (S)	$n - 1$	$= 4$	52.70	13.18	—
Values (A)	$a - 1$	$= 3$	86.60	28.87	2.57
SA	$(a - 1)(n - 1)$	$= 12$	134.90	11.24	—
Total	$an - 1$	$= 19$	274.20		

$an - a - n + 1$. The corrected SS is therefore given by $SS_{SA} = TSS - ASS - SSS + CF = 308.00 - 120.40 - 86.50 + 33.80 = 134.90$.

According to Schultz's rules, the three mean squares contain the following components:

$$1. \quad MS_S = S$$

$$2. \quad MS_A = SA + A$$

$$3. \quad MS_{SA} = SA$$

As presented here, MS_{SA} implies that nonadditivity exists for this design—that is, MS_{SA} represents, in part, an interaction of subjects and treatment. At present, it is sufficient to note that as a result of this nonadditivity, experimental variable A is testable—$F = MS_A/MS_{SA} = 28.87/11.24 = 2.57$ (not significant)—whereas the among subjects variable (S) is not. We are not normally interested in testing S, however, which represents *systematic* differences among subjects. As in the case of the randomized block design (Chapter 7), a value of the SA design is that it permits assessment of a source of variability that can be subtracted from the error term, thereby reducing error and enhancing the likelihood that the F ratio for the experimental variable will prove significant.

The additivity assumption for the SA design states that each dependent score (X, representing the congruence/incongruence of personal values and perceived Republican Administration policy positions) equals the sum of the effects of the main variables, plus the grand mean and error, that is, $X = \mu + S + A + SA$, where SA is assumed to contain residual error only. But because there is only $n = 1$ score per cell in Table 10.1, residual error cannot be measured separately from any interaction that might exist between variables S and A; consequently, the SA term may contain both residual error plus variability arising because of nonadditivity, that is, because of subjects' performances interacting with the A variable.

More specifically, an interaction arises, in part, when one or more subjects' individual performances depart significantly from the mean performances of the group. For example, if, on the average, X scores increase steadily from value W to value B to R and to D, then for additivity to hold, individual subjects would be expected to follow the same course. But it is also possible that some subjects would have high X scores at the outset (condition W), leaving little room for higher scores during subsequent testing. Tukey's test for nonadditivity takes into account both the subject's mean performance over all levels of A and the subject's rate of change relative to the group's rate of change.

Tukey's test for nonadditivity was illustrated previously (Table 7.3 and surrounding text) and, when applied to the data in Table 10.1, shows the additive assumption to be tenable (F_{nonadd} = 1.07, not significant, α = .25). Had the results been otherwise, the data might have required transformation or an adjustment in the procedure for determining the critical F ratio in examining the null hypothesis. There are certain benefits accruing from additivity—for example, it permits a test of the Subjects effect in Table 10.2—but its importance should not be overly stressed insofar as most practical situations are concerned. It is normally simpler to assume the worst (i.e., to assume that nonadditivity exists), and this conservative bias is built into the analysis culminating in Table 10.2, as well as in subsequent analyses.

A related problem in designs involving repeated measures, and which has already been discussed for this entire class of designs (i.e., randomized block designs), is the assumption of sphericity, or circularity. A comparatively simple modification of F testing procedures can compensate for the violation of this assumption (modified from Myers, 1979: 173–174). Table 10.3(a) displays the correlations among the a = 4 treatments (i.e., the four columns of Table 10.1), whereas Table 10.3(b) contains the variances (in parentheses) and covariances. (The covariance between any two levels of variable A is obtained by multiplying their correlation by the product of their respective standard deviations; therefore, for the values of W and B, for example, COV = $(0.13)(\sqrt{2.80})(\sqrt{25.70})$ = 1.10.)

TABLE 10.3

	W	B	R	D		
(a) Correlation matrix						
W	1.00	.13	.35	.85		
B	.13	1.00	−.10	−.08		
R	.35	−.10	1.00	−.11		
D	.85	−.08	−.11	1.00		
(b) Variance-covariance matrix						
W	(2.80)	1.10	2.09	3.40		
B	1.10	(25.70)	−1.82	−0.95		
R	2.09	−1.82	(12.70)	−0.94		
D	3.40	−0.95	0.25	(5.70)		
$\overline{X}$	2.35	6.01	3.31	1.80	3.37	GM
$\overline{X}^2$	5.51	36.09	10.92	3.25	55.77	$\Sigma\overline{X}^2$
					906.58	$\Sigma\Sigma X^2$

The column averages are recorded in row $\overline{X}$ of Table 10.3(b), and the square of the column averages in row $\overline{X}^2$; the average of the column averages (grand mean) is therefore GM $= 3.37$, and the sum of the squared column averages is $\Sigma \overline{X}^2 = 55.77$; the sum of squares of all 16 variances and covariances is $\Sigma\Sigma X^2 = 906.58$. In addition, the average of the four variances is $\overline{S}^2 = \frac{1}{4}(2.80 + 25.70 + 12.70 + 5.70) = 11.73$. The following three calculations are also required:

$$A \quad (\overline{S}^2 - GM)^2 = (11.73 - 3.37)^2 = 69.89$$

$$B \quad 2a\Sigma\overline{X}^2 = (2)(4)(55.77) = 446.16$$

$$C \quad a^2 GM^2 = (16)(3.37)^2 = 181.71$$

An estimated adjustment factor ($\hat{\epsilon}$), to be employed subsequently, is obtained as follows:

$$
\begin{aligned}
\hat{\epsilon} &= \frac{a^2 A}{(a-1)\left(\Sigma X^2 - B + C\right)} \\
&= \frac{(16)(69.89)}{(3)(906.58 - 446.16 + 181.71)} \qquad [10.1] \\
&= 0.58
\end{aligned}
$$

In the case of nonadditivity, the F test in Table 10.2 would still be an exact test so long as the sphericity requirement is met, in which case the adjustment factor would be $\hat{\epsilon} = 1.00$. To compensate for lack of sphericity, the degrees of freedom are modified as a function of $\hat{\epsilon}$. As shown in Table 10.2, $df_A = 3$ and $df_{SA} = 12$ are the numerator and denominator degrees of freedom, respectively, used in entering the F table (Appendix B), which indicates that the calculated F must exceed $F_{3,12} = 3.49$ in order to be significant at the $\alpha = .05$ level. Given that $\hat{\epsilon} = 0.58$, which reflects the magnitude of variance-covariance heterogeneity, the above degrees of freedom are adjusted as follows:

$$df'_A = \hat{\epsilon}(df_A) = 0.58(3) = 1.74 \simeq 2$$

$$df'_{SA} = \hat{\epsilon}(df_{SA}) = 0.58(12) = 6.97 \simeq 7$$

The adjusted df' are rounded to the nearest whole number (2 and 7, respectively), and the corrected values now indicate that the calculated F must exceed $F_{2,7} = 4.74$ in order to be significant at the $\alpha = .05$ level.

The Geisser-Greenhouse correction (Keppel, 1982: 470-471) always adopts an adjustment factor of $\hat{\epsilon} = 1/(a-1)$—in this case $1/3 = 0.33$—

TABLE 10.4

Subjects	Party (A)								
	Republican				Democratic				
	Values (B)								
	W	B	R	D	W	B	R	D	Sum
S1	1	4	0	−1	−3	2	2	0	5
S2	2	−8	2	1	2	6	−2	4	7
S3	2	−7	1	2	2	7	−2	0	5
S4	0	−5	−7	1	3	7	9	2	10
S5	−2	−8	0	−4	1	10	0	4	1
Sum	3	−24	−4	−1	5	32	7	10	28 Sum
									.70 GM
									702 TSS

which is the smallest possible value of $\hat{\epsilon}$ and therefore the most conservative adjustment (albeit the simplest to calculate) that can be made. Given $\hat{\epsilon} = 0.33$, the degrees of freedom of $df'_A = 1$ and $df'_{SA} = 4$ would require a calculated F in excess of $F_{1,4} = 7.71$ in order to reach significance at the $\alpha = .05$ level.

The SAB variant of the repeated measures design, as shown in Table 10.4, involves the cross-classification of three variables: A, B, and S (subjects). In this case, subjects were asked to assess the extent to which the current Republican Administration favored certain policies (representative of the same four values in Table 10.1), but in addition to assess the extent to which a Democratic Administration would favor the same policies were it in power. As previously, the dependent variable represents the congruence or incongruence of each subject's own assessment of personal cost/benefit and the subject's perception of the parties' policy positions.

Table 10.5 shows the sources of variance associated with the SAB-type design, as well as the general df, which will always be the same regardless of the sizes of a, b, or n (assuming equal ns per AB groups). In this instance, as before, the among-subjects (S) df and the within-subjects (WS) df sum to total df, and the same applies for the sums of squares. There is usually no interest in the overall WS effect, however, because it is broken down into six components—A, B, and AB interaction, plus three error terms (SA, SB, and SAB).

The expanded df reveal eight unique symbols and symbol combinations which, when decoded, produce the following uncorrected SS (based on the data in Table 10.4):

TABLE 10.5

	Degrees of Freedom			
SV	General	Expanded	SS	MS
S	$n - 1$	$=$ (4) $= n - 1$	(5.40)	1.35
WS	$n(ab - 1)$	$=$ (35) $= abn - n$	(677.00)	19.34
A	$a - 1$	$=$ 1 $= a - 1$	160.00	160.00
SA	$(a - 1)(n - 1)$	$=$ 4 $= ab - a - n + 1$	105.50	26.38
B	$b - 1$	$=$ 3 $= b - 1$	2.20	0.73
SB	$(b - 1)(n - 1)$	$=$ 12 $= bn - b - n + 1$	43.80	3.65
AB	$(a - 1)(b - 1)$	$=$ 3 $= ab - a - b + 1$	178.20	59.40
SAB	$(a - 1)(b - 1)(n - 1) =$	12 $= abn - ab - an + a$ $- bn + b + n - 1$	187.30	15.61
Total	$abn - 1$	$=$ (39) $= abn - 1$	(682.40)	

$$1 = \text{CF} = \tfrac{1}{40}(28)^2 = 19.60$$

$$n = \text{SSS} = \tfrac{1}{8}(5^2 + 7^2 + 5^2 + 10^2 + 1^2) = 25.00$$

$$abn = \text{TSS} = 1^2 + 2^2 + \cdots + 2^2 + 4^2 = 702.00$$

$$a = \text{ASS} = \tfrac{1}{20}\big[(3 - 24 - 4 - 1)^2$$
$$+ (5 + 32 + 7 + 10)^2\big] = 179.60$$

$$an = \text{ANSS} = \tfrac{1}{4}\big[(1 + 4 + 0 - 1)^2 + \cdots$$
$$+ (1 + 10 + 0 + 4)^2\big] = 290.50$$

$$b = \text{BSS} = \tfrac{1}{10}\big[(3 + 5)^2 + \cdots + (\{-1\} + 10)^2\big] = 21.80$$

$$bn = \text{BNSS} = \tfrac{1}{2}\big[(1 + \{-3\})^2 + \cdots + (\{-4\} + 4)^2\big] = 71.00$$

$$ab = \text{ABSS} = \tfrac{1}{5}\big[(3)^2 + (-24)^2 + \cdots + (10)^2\big] = 360.00$$

an and *bn* are perhaps the least obvious components. Decoded, the former reads as follows:

$$an = \text{ANSS} = \frac{1}{b}\underset{a}{\sum}\underset{n}{\sum}\left(\underset{b}{\sum}X\right)^2$$
$$= \tfrac{1}{4}\big[(A_1B_1S_1 + A_1B_2S_1 + A_1B_3S_1 + A_1B_4S_1)^2$$
$$+ \cdots + (A_2B_1S_5 + A_2B_2S_5 + A_2B_3S_5 + A_2B_4S_5)^2\big]$$
$$= \tfrac{1}{4}\big[(1 + 4 + 0 + \{-1\})^2 + \cdots + (1 + 10 + 0 + 4)^2\big]$$
$$= 290.50$$

That is, the levels of B are summed while the levels of A and S remain constant. Similarly for bn:

$$
\begin{aligned}
bn = \text{BNSS} &= \frac{1}{a}\Big[(A_1B_1S_1 + A_2B_1S_1)^2 + (A_1B_1S_2 + A_2B_1S_2)^2 \\
&\quad + \cdots + (A_1B_4S_5 + A_2B_4S_5)^2\Big] \\
&= \tfrac{1}{2}\Big[(1 + \{-3\})^2 + (2 + 2)^2 + \cdots \\
&\quad + (\{-4\} + 4)^2\Big] \\
&= 71.00
\end{aligned}
$$

By this point it should be clear that calculations of the uncorrected SS merely indicate different ways to cut the cake represented by the matrix of raw scores: The squares of the row totals, when summed, reflect differences among subjects (SSS); columns one through four squared, when compared with columns five through eight squared, reflect differences between the levels of variable A (ASS); columns one and five versus two and six versus three and seven, etc. contrast levels of B (BSS); and so forth, each SS being divided by the number of scores entering into each sum.

The expanded df in Table 10.5 show how to combine the various uncorrected SS in order to calculate the corrected SS. The mean squares, as usual, are obtained by $\text{MS} = \text{SS}/\text{df}$. The mean square for within subjects (WS) is of no importance because interest normally focuses on the various components (A, B, AB) into which the WS variability can be divided.

It remains only to form the correct F ratios, and this, as shown previously, depends on whether the components represent fixed or random effects. Table 10.6 displays the results of two situations: SAB, in which A and B are both fixed effects (S is always a random variable); and SAB', a mixed design in which A is fixed (i.e., experimental interest is in the responses to the Republican and Democratic alternatives only) and B' is random (i.e., the four values—W, B, R, and D—are only randomly selected from a larger universe to which any conclusions will be generalized). As is indicated, the calculations of SS and MS remain the same in both SAB and SAB', although the ways in which the mean squares are combined in the F ratios differ.

Before proceeding, note that nonadditivity will be assumed in both instances (i.e., that the SAB and SAB' components represent a confounding of random influences plus the interaction of subjects with AB combi-

TABLE 10.6

(a) Fixed effects model (SAB)

SV	MS	Mean Square Components	F Ratios	
1 S	1.35	S	—	
WS	19.34	—	—	
2 A	160.00	$SA + A$	$\frac{2}{3}$	6.07
3 SA	26.38	SA	—	—
4 B	0.73	$SB + B$	$\frac{4}{5}$	0.20
5 SB	3.65	SB	—	—
6 AB	59.40	$SAB + AB$	$\frac{6}{7}$	3.81*
7 SAB	15.61	SAB		
Total				

(b) Mixed effects model (SAB')

SV	MS	MS Components	F Ratios	
1 S	1.35	$SB' + S$	$\frac{1}{5}$	0.37
WS	19.34	—	—	
2 A	160.00	$SAB' + AB' + SA + A$	$2/(3 + 6 - 7)$	2.28
3 SA	26.38	$SAB' + SA$	$\frac{3}{7}$	1.69
4 B	0.73	$SB' + B'$	$\frac{4}{5}$	0.20
5 SB	3.65	SB'	—	—
6 AB	59.40	$SAB' + AB'$	$\frac{6}{7}$	3.81*
7 SAB	15.61	SAB'		
Total				

*$p < .05$

nations), although in practical situations it would be wise to test for nonaddivity because there are certain advantages that accrue if additivity does in fact pertain. With nonadditivity, it may also be necessary to modify F testing procedures when the sphericity assumption is violated (see Table 10.3). Were the Geisser-Greenhouse strategy to be employed, therefore, $\hat{\epsilon} = 1/(a - 1)$ or $1/(b - 1)$ would be used as the adjustment factors for the A or B variables, respectively—and for the AB interaction.

The A effect for the SAB' design is the most complicated and serves to illustrate the testing principles involved. According to Schultz's rules, MS_A contains within it variance components $SAB' + AB' + SA + A$, that is, the variability associated with the levels of A itself, plus variability associated with those other components containing A in which all other included factors are random. Because there is no other MS that contains all of the components in MS_A except for A itself, it is necessary to piece together a quasi-F, in this case $MS_A/(MS_{SA} + MS_{AB'} - MS_{SAB'})$, which produces the following ratio:

$$F_1 = \frac{SAB' + AB' + SA + A}{(SAB' + SA) + (SAB' + AB') - SAB'}$$
$$= \frac{SAB' + AB' + SA + A}{SAB' + AB' + SA}$$

There are sometimes alternative quasi-F ratios that can be constructed, as for example $(MS_A + MS_{SAB'})/(MS_{AB'} + MS_{SA})$, which produces

$$F_2 = \frac{(SAB' + AB' + SA + A) + SAB'}{(SAB' + AB') + (SAB' + SA)}$$
$$= \frac{SAB' + SAB' + AB' + SA + A}{SAB' + SAB' + AB' + SA}$$

F_1 and F_2 display the necessary property that all the terms in the numerator are contained in the denominator except for the term being tested (in this case A). Numerically, the F ratios are:

$$F_1 = \frac{MS_A}{MS_{SA} + MS_{AB'} - MS_{SAB'}}$$
$$= \frac{160}{26.38 + 59.40 - 15.61} = 2.28$$

$$F_2 = \frac{MS_A + MS_{SAB'}}{MS_{AB'} + MS_{SA}}$$
$$= \frac{160 + 15.61}{59.40 + 26.38} = 2.05$$

It is perhaps worth noting that it is possible for the quasi-F to be negative, a computational possibility which is theoretically senseless.

There are $a - 1 = 1$ df associated with the numerator of the quasi-F_1 ratio, but it remains to determine the number of df associated with the denominator. According to Keppel (1982: 330–333), the df for a combination of mean squares (involving $MS_1, MS_2, \ldots , MS_k$) is obtained as follows:

$$df = \frac{(MS_1 \pm \cdots \pm MS_k)^2}{(MS_1^2/df_1) + \cdots + (MS_k^2/df_k)} \quad [10.1]$$

In the case of the variance components involved in variable A in Tables 10.5 and 10.6(b), the df for the denominator of the F_1 ratio are calculated as follows:

$$
df = \frac{MS_{SA} + MS_{AB'} - MS_{SAB'}}{(MS_{SA}^2/df_{SA}) + (MS_{AB'}^2/df_{AB'}) + (MS_{SAB'}^2/df_{SAB'})}
$$

$$
= \frac{26.38 + 59.40 - 15.61}{(26.38^2/4) + (59.40^2/3) + (15.61^2/12)}
$$

$$
= 3.59 \simeq 4
$$

The result is rounded to the nearest whole number. The tabular $F_{.05;1,4} = 7.71$ indicates that the calculated $F = 2.28$ is not significant.

In the case of quasi-F_2 above, df must be calculated for the numerator and denominator because both are composites. These calculations are left as an exercise, which should produce 1.20 and 5.45 for the numerator and denominator df, respectively. Rounded to 1 and 5, the tabular $F_{.05;1,5} = 6.61$ indicates that the calculated F still falls short of significance.

In the SA and SAB designs illustrated above, no distinctions were made between subjects, but in Table 10.7 a distinction is made between subjects assessed as democratic versus undemocratic in attitude. (As was the case with the gender variable in Chapter 9, attitude is a subject trait rather than an experimental variable.) The between-subjects variable is therefore cross-classified factorially with the within-subjects variable, with $n = 2$ subjects (in this instance) being nested within each of the two levels of A, but all subjects being exposed to all four levels of B—hence the designation $S(A)B$. This is referred to generically as a *mixed design*, and it gives rise to two different sources of error variance—between subjects (BS) and within subjects (WS).

TABLE 10.7

Attitude (A)	Trials (B)				Row Sum	Type Sum
	1^+	2°	3^+	4°		
(A1)	5	6	6	7	24	41
Democratic	4	4	6	3	17	
(A2)	−1	−2	−5	−3	−11	−24
Nondemocratic	−4	0	−4	−5	−13	
Sum	4	8	3	2	17	Sum
					319	TSS

The experiment consisted of presenting subjects with 100 cards, on each of which was a set of pronouns (I, you, he, she, it, we, they), an infinitive (e.g., "to throw"), and an object (e.g., "the ball"). Each subject's task was to select a pronoun, match it with the correct form of the verb, and read the sentence aloud—for example, "He threw the ball." During the first 20 readings, a count was made of the number of times the subject used first-person pronouns "I" or "we" in a sentence (operant level). During the second 20 readings, the subject was given a social reinforcement (e.g., "good," "uh-huh") for each first-person pronoun used. The figures in column 1^+ indicate the number of first-person pronouns expressed by each subject over and above his or her operant level. In trials $2°$ and $4°$ (20 cards each) no reinforcement was given for selecting first-person pronouns; in trial 3^+, as in 1^+, reinforcement was given. The theory proposed that persons with democratic inclinations are more adaptable to subtle social cues. Under the null hypothesis, therefore, it would be expected that democratic subjects would respond to social reinforcements by expressing larger numbers of reinforced responses (in this case first-person pronouns).

As shown in Table 10.8, the sums of squares for between subjects (SS_{BS}) and within subjects (SS_{WS}) add to the total SS. In turn, SS_{BS} is divided into SS_A and $SS_{S(A)}$, that is, into the sums of squares attributable to differences between the two different attitude types and among subjects nested within levels of A. The SS_{WS} is divided into sums of squares attributable to performance differences among trials, to differences among AB cells (interaction), and to differences arising because of the interaction of subjects with variable B within levels of variable A ($SS_{S(A)B}$).

The formulas required to calculate the sums of squares are straightforward and should by now be obvious; they are therefore left as an exercise.

TABLE 10.8

SV	df		SS	MS	F
BS	$an - 1$	$= 3$	(270.69)		
A (Attitude)	$a - 1$	$= 1$	264.06	264.06	79.72*
$S(A)$	$a(n - 1)$	$= 2$	6.63	3.31	
WS	$an(b - 1)$	$= 12$	(30.25)		
B (Trials)	$b - 1$	$= 3$	5.19	1.73	0.81
AB	$(a - 1)(b - 1)$	$= 3$	12.19	4.06	1.89
$S(A)B$	$a(b - 1)(n - 1)$	$= 6$	12.88	2.15	
Total	$abn - 1$	$= 15$	(300.94)		

*$p < .05$

Similarly, the application of Schultz's rules for determining valid F ratios should also be routine: The ratios shown in Table 10.8 assume a fixed effects model, but the proper ratios would be somewhat different were either A or B a random variable.

The A effect is significant, and inspection of the data in Table 10.7 indicates that the subjects assessed as democratic responded to social reinforcements by emitting larger numbers of reinforced responses, whereas the nondemocratic responded with fewer. Because there are only $a = 2$ levels of A, both a priori and a posteriori testing as well as trend testing are superfluous. With $a > 2$, however, such testing would be in order and the standard error for the a posteriori testing of means, using Tukey's HSD test (see expression 6.5), would be

$$S_{\overline{X}_A} = \sqrt{MS_{S(A)}/bn}$$

which in the above example would be

$$S_{\overline{X}_A} = \sqrt{3.31/8} = 0.64$$

By the same token, a test of a significant Trials effect (variable B) would involve the error term associated with within-subjects differences:

$$S_{\overline{X}_B} = \sqrt{MS_{S(A)B}/an} = \sqrt{2.15/4} = 0.73$$

Similarly, in the use of Scheffé's or of a priori testing, care must be taken to utilize that error term associated with the effect being tested.

Testing is more complicated in the case of a significant interaction. The AB interaction in Table 10.8 is not significant; if it were, however, it would indicate differences in the levels of one variable at various levels of the other—for example, that the pattern of scores at $B1$, $B2$, $B3$, and $B4$ were different at $A1$ than at $A2$. In terms of Table 10.7, this would require testing the differences among the B means at $A1$ and again at $A2$, or testing the differences between $A1$ and $A2$ at the four levels of B. (To guard against Type I errors, only one of these sets of analyses would be undertaken.) Because A is a between-subjects variable and B a within-subjects variable, the testing of levels of A at each level of B involves both between- and within-subjects error, hence it is necessary to calculate a composite mean square (MS_{comp}) based on the figures in Table 10.8:

$$MS_{comp} = \frac{SS_{S(A)} + SS_{S(A)B}}{df_{S(A)} + df_{S(A)B}} \qquad [10.2]$$

$$= \frac{6.63 + 12.88}{2 + 6} = 2.44$$

The standard error for testing mean differences using Tukey's HSD test is

$$S_{\bar{X}_{AB}} = \sqrt{MS_{comp}/n}$$
$$= \sqrt{2.44/2} = 1.10$$

The degrees of freedom would also have to be pooled, as follows:

$$df_{pooled} = \frac{(SS_{S(A)} + SS_{S(A)B})^2}{(SS_{S(A)})^2/df_{S(A)} + (SS_{S(A)B})^2/df_{S(A)B}}$$

$$= \frac{(6.63 + 12.88)^2}{(6.63)^2/2 + (12.88)^2/6} \qquad [10.3]$$

$$= 7.67$$

The pooled df are rounded to the nearest whole number (df = 8 in this case), and the testing then proceeds as outlined in section 6.4.

If the levels of B had been examined at A_1 and again at A_2, then $MS_{S(A)B}$ would have been sufficient as an error term. The difference here, although perhaps not obvious from the computational formulas, is that the B comparisons (at the various levels of A) employ only sums of squares that are derived from within-subjects sources of variance, whereas the A comparisons (at the various levels of B) employ both between- and within-subjects sources. The general principles behind the derivations of these procedures for analyzing interactions in mixed designs are presented in detail in Howell (1987) and Kirk (1982).

The repeated measures and mixed designs, as was the case with the factorial design, are capable of being extended ad infinitum with additional between-subjects and within-subjects variables, although larger designs require considerably greater numbers of subjects and produce higher-order interactions which, if significant, are usually difficult to interpret. This type of design is especially useful when relatively small numbers of subjects are available, when it is desirable to examine the behavior of individuals under a variety of treatments and treatment combinations, and in those cases in which duration plays an important role. Examples of the latter include the many learning experiments in which subjects' abilities to master various tasks are repeatedly examined across several trials.

APPENDIX A
Percentage Points of *t* Distribution (2-Tailed)

df	alpha .05	alpha .01	df	alpha .05	alpha .01
1	12.71	63.66	22	2.08	2.82
2	4.31	9.93	24	2.07	2.80
3	3.19	5.85	26	2.06	2.78
4	2.78	4.61	28	2.05	2.77
5	2.58	4.04	30	2.05	2.75
6	2.45	3.71	40	2.03	2.71
7	2.37	3.45	50	2.01	2.68
8	2.31	3.36	60	2.00	2.66
9	2.27	3.25	80	1.99	2.64
10	2.23	3.17	100	1.99	2.63
11	2.21	3.11	200	1.98	2.61
12	2.18	3.06	400	1.97	2.59
13	2.16	3.02	∞	1.96	2.58
14	2.15	2.98			
15	2.14	2.95			
16	2.12	2.93			
17	2.11	2.90			
18	2.11	2.88			
19	2.10	2.87			
20	2.09	2.85			

NOTE: Table values calculated by the authors.

APPENDIX B
Upper Percentage Points of F Distribution

df denom- inator	df numerator 1	2	3	alpha = .05 4	5	6	7	8	9	10
1	161.4	199.5	215.8	224.8	230.0	233.8	236.5	238.6	240.1	242.1
2	18.51	19.00	19.16	19.25	19.30	19.33	19.35	19.37	19.38	19.40
3	10.13	9.55	9.28	9.12	9.01	8.94	8.89	8.85	8.81	8.79
4	7.71	6.94	6.59	6.39	6.26	6.16	6.09	6.04	6.00	5.96
5	6.61	5.79	5.41	5.19	5.05	4.95	4.88	4.82	4.77	4.74
6	5.99	5.14	4.76	4.53	4.39	4.28	4.21	4.15	4.10	4.06
7	5.59	4.74	4.35	4.12	3.97	3.87	3.79	3.73	3.68	3.64
8	5.32	4.46	4.07	3.84	3.69	3.58	3.50	3.44	3.39	3.35
9	5.12	4.26	3.86	3.63	3.48	3.37	3.29	3.23	3.18	3.14
10	4.96	4.10	3.71	3.48	3.33	3.22	3.14	3.07	3.02	2.98
11	4.84	3.98	3.59	3.36	3.20	3.09	3.01	2.95	2.90	2.85
12	4.75	3.89	3.49	3.26	3.11	3.00	2.91	2.85	2.80	2.75
13	4.67	3.81	3.41	3.18	3.03	2.92	2.83	2.77	2.71	2.67
14	4.60	3.74	3.34	3.11	2.96	2.85	2.76	2.70	2.65	2.60
15	4.54	3.68	3.29	3.06	2.90	2.79	2.71	2.64	2.59	2.54
16	4.49	3.63	3.24	3.01	2.85	2.74	2.66	2.59	2.54	2.49
17	4.45	3.59	3.20	2.96	2.81	2.70	2.61	2.55	2.49	2.45
18	4.41	3.55	3.16	2.93	2.77	2.66	2.58	2.51	2.46	2.41
19	4.38	3.52	3.13	2.90	2.74	2.63	2.54	2.48	2.42	2.38
20	4.35	3.49	3.10	2.87	2.71	2.60	2.51	2.45	2.39	2.35
22	4.30	3.44	3.05	2.82	2.66	2.55	2.46	2.40	2.34	2.30
24	4.26	3.40	3.01	2.78	2.62	2.51	2.42	2.36	2.30	2.25
26	4.23	3.37	2.98	2.74	2.59	2.47	2.39	2.32	2.27	2.22
28	4.20	3.34	2.95	2.71	2.56	2.45	2.36	2.29	2.24	2.19
30	4.17	3.32	2.92	2.69	2.53	2.42	2.33	2.27	2.21	2.16
40	4.08	3.23	2.84	2.61	2.45	2.34	2.25	2.18	2.12	2.08
60	4.00	3.15	2.76	2.53	2.37	2.25	2.17	2.10	2.04	1.99
120	3.92	3.07	2.68	2.45	2.29	2.18	2.09	2.02	1.96	1.91
500	3.86	3.01	2.62	2.39	2.23	2.12	2.03	1.96	1.90	1.85
1000	3.85	3.01	2.61	2.38	2.22	2.11	2.02	1.95	1.89	1.84

alpha = .01

	1	2	3	4	5	6	7	8	9	10
1	4048	4993	5377	5577	5668	5924	5992	6096	6132	6168
2	98.50	99.01	99.15	99.23	99.30	99.33	99.35	99.39	99.40	99.43
3	34.12	30.82	29.46	28.71	28.24	27.91	27.67	27.49	27.34	27.23
4	21.20	18.00	16.69	15.98	15.52	15.21	14.98	14.80	14.66	14.55
5	16.26	13.27	12.06	11.39	10.97	10.67	10.46	10.29	10.16	10.05
6	13.75	10.92	9.78	9.15	8.75	8.47	8.26	8.10	7.98	7.87
7	12.25	9.55	8.45	7.85	7.46	7.19	6.99	6.84	6.72	6.62
8	11.26	8.65	7.59	7.01	6.63	6.37	6.18	6.03	5.91	5.81
9	10.56	8.02	6.99	6.42	6.06	5.80	5.61	5.47	5.35	5.26
10	10.04	7.56	6.55	5.99	5.64	5.39	5.20	5.06	4.94	4.85
11	9.65	7.21	6.22	5.67	5.32	5.07	4.89	4.74	4.63	4.54
12	9.33	6.93	5.95	5.41	5.06	4.82	4.64	4.50	4.39	4.30
13	9.07	6.70	5.74	5.21	4.86	4.62	4.44	4.30	4.19	4.10
14	8.86	6.51	5.56	5.04	4.69	4.46	4.28	4.14	4.03	3.94
15	8.68	6.36	5.42	4.89	4.56	4.32	4.14	4.00	3.89	3.80
16	8.53	6.23	5.29	4.77	4.44	4.20	4.03	3.89	3.78	3.69
17	8.40	6.11	5.18	4.67	4.34	4.10	3.93	3.79	3.68	3.59
18	8.29	6.01	5.09	4.58	4.25	4.01	3.84	3.71	3.60	3.51
19	8.18	5.93	5.01	4.50	4.17	3.94	3.77	3.63	3.52	3.43
20	8.10	5.85	4.94	4.43	4.10	3.87	3.70	3.56	3.46	3.37
22	7.95	5.72	4.82	4.31	3.99	3.76	3.59	3.45	3.35	3.26
24	7.82	5.61	4.72	4.22	3.90	3.67	3.50	3.36	3.26	3.17
26	7.72	5.53	4.64	4.14	3.82	3.59	3.42	3.29	3.18	3.09
28	7.64	5.45	4.57	4.07	3.75	3.53	3.36	3.23	3.12	3.03
30	7.56	5.39	4.51	4.02	3.70	3.47	3.30	3.17	3.07	2.98
40	7.31	5.18	4.31	3.83	3.51	3.29	3.12	2.99	2.89	2.80
60	7.08	4.98	4.13	3.65	3.34	3.12	2.95	2.82	2.72	2.63
120	6.85	4.79	3.95	3.48	3.17	2.96	2.79	2.66	2.56	2.47
500	6.69	4.65	3.82	3.36	3.05	2.84	2.68	2.55	2.44	2.36
1000	6.67	4.63	3.80	3.34	3.04	2.82	2.66	2.53	2.43	2.34

SOURCE: Adapted from Howell (1987: Appendix F, pp. 577–579)

APPENDIX C
Upper Percentage Points of the F_{max} Statistic

df= n-1	df=g 2	3	4	5	6	7	8	9	10
				alpha = .05					
2	39.0	87.5	142	202	266	333	403	475	550
3	15.4	27.8	39.2	50.7	62.0	72.9	83.5	93.9	104
4	9.60	15.5	20.6	25.2	29.5	33.6	37.5	41.1	44.6
5	7.15	10.8	13.7	16.3	18.7	20.8	22.9	24.7	26.5
6	5.82	8.38	10.4	12.1	13.7	15.0	16.3	17.5	18.6
7	4.99	6.94	8.44	9.70	10.8	11.8	12.7	13.5	14.3
8	4.43	6.00	7.18	8.12	9.03	9.78	10.5	11.1	11.7
9	4.03	5.34	6.31	7.11	7.80	8.41	8.95	9.45	9.91
10	3.72	4.85	5.67	6.34	6.92	7.42	7.87	8.28	8.66
12	3.28	4.16	4.79	5.30	5.72	6.09	6.42	6.72	7.00
15	2.86	3.54	4.01	4.37	4.68	4.95	5.19	5.40	5.59
20	2.46	2.95	3.29	3.54	3.76	3.94	4.10	4.24	4.37
30	2.07	2.40	2.61	2.78	2.91	3.02	3.12	3.21	3.29
60	1.67	1.85	1.96	2.04	2.11	2.17	2.22	2.26	2.30
∞	1.00	1.00	1.00	1.00	1.00	1.00	1.00	1.00	1.00

SOURCE: *Biometrika Tables for Statisticians* (3rd ed., Vol. 1, Table 31) edited by E. S. Pearson and H. O. Hartley, 1966, New York: Cambridge University Press. Reproduced by the kind permission of the trustees of *Biometrika*.

APPENDIX D
Studentized Range (Tukey's HSD Test)

alpha = .05

df error	range (r) 2	3	4	5	6	7	8	9	10
1	18.0	27.0	32.8	37.1	40.4	43.1	45.4	47.4	49.1
2	6.09	8.3	9.8	10.9	11.7	12.4	13.0	13.5	14.0
3	4.50	5.91	6.82	7.50	8.04	8.48	8.85	9.18	9.46
4	3.93	5.04	5.76	6.29	6.71	7.05	7.35	7.60	7.83
5	3.64	4.60	5.22	5.67	6.03	6.33	6.58	6.80	6.99
6	3.46	4.34	4.90	5.31	5.63	5.89	6.12	6.32	6.49
7	3.34	4.16	4.68	5.06	5.36	5.61	5.82	6.00	6.16
8	3.26	4.04	4.53	4.89	5.17	5.40	5.60	5.77	5.92
9	3.20	3.95	4.42	4.76	5.02	5.24	5.43	5.60	5.74
10	3.15	3.88	4.33	4.65	4.91	5.12	5.30	5.46	5.60
11	3.11	3.82	4.26	4.57	4.82	5.03	5.20	5.35	5.49
12	3.08	3.77	4.20	4.51	4.75	4.95	5.12	5.27	5.40
13	3.06	3.73	4.15	4.45	4.69	4.88	5.05	5.19	5.32
14	3.03	3.70	4.11	4.41	4.64	4.83	4.99	5.13	5.25
15	3.01	3.67	4.08	4.37	4.60	4.78	4.94	5.08	5.20
16	3.00	3.65	4.05	4.33	4.56	4.74	4.90	5.03	5.15
17	2.98	3.63	4.02	4.30	4.52	4.71	4.86	4.99	5.11
18	2.97	3.61	4.00	4.28	4.49	4.67	4.82	4.96	5.07
19	2.96	3.59	3.98	4.25	4.47	4.65	4.79	4.92	5.04
20	2.95	3.58	3.96	4.23	4.45	4.62	4.77	4.90	5.01
24	2.92	3.53	3.90	4.17	4.37	4.54	4.68	4.81	4.92
30	2.89	3.49	3.84	4.10	4.30	4.46	4.60	4.72	4.83
40	2.86	3.44	3.79	4.04	4.23	4.39	4.52	4.63	4.74
60	2.83	3.40	3.74	3.98	4.16	4.31	4.44	4.55	4.65
120	2.80	3.36	3.69	3.92	4.10	4.24	4.36	4.48	4.56
∞	2.77	3.31	3.63	3.86	4.03	4.17	4.29	4.39	4.47

alpha = .01

df error	2	3	4	5	6	7	8	9	10
1	90.0	135	164	186	202	216	227	237	246
2	14.0	19.0	22.3	24.7	26.6	28.2	29.5	30.7	31.7
3	8.26	10.6	12.2	13.3	14.2	15.0	15.6	16.2	16.7
4	6.51	8.12	9.17	9.96	10.6	11.1	11.5	11.9	12.3
5	5.70	6.97	7.80	8.42	8.91	9.32	9.67	9.97	10.24
6	5.24	6.33	7.03	7.56	7.97	8.32	8.61	8.87	9.10
7	4.95	5.92	6.54	7.01	7.37	7.68	7.94	8.17	8.37
8	4.74	5.63	6.20	6.63	6.96	7.24	7.47	7.68	7.87
9	4.60	5.43	5.96	6.35	6.66	6.91	7.13	7.32	7.49
10	4.48	5.27	5.77	6.14	6.43	6.67	6.87	7.05	7.21
11	4.39	5.14	5.62	5.97	6.25	6.48	6.67	6.84	6.99
12	4.32	5.04	5.50	5.84	6.10	6.32	6.51	6.67	6.81
13	4.26	4.96	5.40	5.73	5.98	6.19	6.37	6.53	6.67
14	4.21	4.89	5.32	5.63	5.88	6.08	6.26	6.41	6.54
15	4.17	4.83	5.25	5.56	5.80	5.99	6.16	6.31	6.44
16	4.13	4.78	5.19	5.49	5.72	5.92	6.08	6.22	6.35
17	4.10	4.74	5.14	5.43	5.66	5.85	6.01	6.15	6.27
18	4.07	4.70	5.09	5.38	5.60	5.79	5.94	6.08	6.20
19	4.05	4.67	5.05	5.33	5.55	5.73	5.89	6.02	6.14
20	4.02	4.64	5.02	5.29	5.51	5.69	5.84	5.97	6.09
24	3.96	4.54	4.91	5.17	5.37	5.54	5.69	5.81	5.92
30	3.89	4.45	4.80	5.05	5.24	5.40	5.54	5.65	5.76
40	3.82	4.37	4.70	4.93	5.11	5.27	5.39	5.50	5.60
60	3.76	4.28	4.60	4.82	4.99	5.13	5.25	5.36	5.45
120	3.70	4.20	4.50	4.71	4.87	5.01	5.12	5.21	5.30
∞	3.64	4.12	4.40	4.60	4.76	4.88	4.99	5.08	5.16

SOURCE: *Biometrika Tables for Statisticians* (3rd ed., Vol. 1, Table 29) edited by E. S. Pearson and H. O. Hartley, 1966, New York: Cambridge University Press. Reproduced by the kind permission of the trustees of *Biometrika*.

APPENDIX E
t_D Distribution (Dunn's Test)

df error	No. of comparisons 2	3	4	5	6	7	8	9	10
					alpha = .05				
5	3.16	3.53	3.81	4.03	4.22	4.38	4.53	4.66	4.77
6	2.97	3.29	3.52	3.71	3.86	4.00	4.12	4.22	4.32
7	2.84	3.13	3.34	3.50	3.64	3.75	3.86	3.95	4.03
8	2.75	3.02	3.21	3.36	3.48	3.58	3.68	3.76	3.83
9	2.69	2.93	3.11	3.25	3.36	3.46	3.55	3.62	3.69
10	2.63	2.87	3.04	3.17	3.28	3.37	3.45	3.52	3.58
11	2.59	2.82	2.98	3.11	3.21	3.29	3.37	3.44	3.50
12	2.56	2.78	2.93	3.05	3.15	3.24	3.31	3.37	3.43
13	2.53	2.75	2.90	3.01	3.11	3.19	3.26	3.32	3.37
14	2.51	2.72	2.86	2.98	3.07	3.15	3.21	3.27	3.33
15	2.49	2.69	2.84	2.95	3.04	3.11	3.18	3.23	3.29
16	2.47	2.67	2.81	2.92	3.01	3.08	3.15	3.20	3.25
17	2.46	2.65	2.79	2.90	2.98	3.06	3.12	3.17	3.22
18	2.45	2.64	2.77	2.88	2.96	3.03	3.09	3.15	3.20
19	2.43	2.63	2.76	2.86	2.94	3.01	3.07	3.13	3.17
20	2.42	2.61	2.74	2.85	2.93	3.00	3.06	3.11	3.15
21	2.41	2.60	2.73	2.83	2.91	2.98	3.04	3.09	3.14
22	2.41	2.59	2.72	2.82	2.90	2.97	3.02	3.07	3.12
23	2.40	2.58	2.71	2.81	2.89	2.95	3.01	3.06	3.10
24	2.39	2.57	2.70	2.80	2.88	2.94	3.00	3.05	3.09
25	2.38	2.57	2.69	2.79	2.86	2.93	2.99	3.03	3.08
30	2.36	2.54	2.66	2.75	2.82	2.89	2.94	2.99	3.03
40	2.33	2.50	2.62	2.70	2.78	2.84	2.89	2.93	2.97
50	2.31	2.48	2.59	2.68	2.75	2.81	2.85	2.90	2.94
75	2.29	2.45	2.56	2.64	2.71	2.77	2.81	2.86	2.89
100	2.28	2.43	2.54	2.63	2.69	2.75	2.79	2.83	2.87
∞	2.24	2.39	2.50	2.58	2.64	2.69	2.73	2.77	2.81
					alpha = .01				
5	4.77	5.25	5.60	5.89	6.14	6.35	6.54	6.71	6.87
6	4.32	4.70	4.98	5.21	5.40	5.56	5.71	5.84	5.96
7	4.03	4.36	4.59	4.79	4.94	5.08	5.20	5.31	5.41
8	3.83	4.12	4.33	4.50	4.64	4.76	4.86	4.96	5.04
9	3.69	3.95	4.15	4.30	4.42	4.53	4.62	4.71	4.78
10	3.58	3.83	4.00	4.14	4.26	4.36	4.44	4.52	4.59
11	3.50	3.73	3.89	4.02	4.13	4.22	4.30	4.37	4.44
12	3.43	3.65	3.81	3.93	4.03	4.12	4.19	4.26	4.32
13	3.37	3.58	3.73	3.85	3.95	4.03	4.10	4.16	4.22
14	3.33	3.53	3.67	3.79	3.88	3.96	4.03	4.09	4.14
15	3.29	3.48	3.62	3.73	3.82	3.90	3.96	4.02	4.07
16	3.25	3.44	3.58	3.69	3.77	3.85	3.91	3.96	4.01
17	3.22	3.41	3.54	3.65	3.73	3.80	3.86	3.92	3.97
18	3.20	3.38	3.51	3.61	3.69	3.76	3.82	3.87	3.92
19	3.17	3.35	3.48	3.58	3.66	3.73	3.79	3.84	3.88
20	3.15	3.33	3.46	3.55	3.63	3.70	3.75	3.80	3.85
21	3.14	3.31	3.43	3.53	3.60	3.67	3.73	3.78	3.82
22	3.12	3.29	3.41	3.50	3.58	3.64	3.70	3.75	3.79
23	3.10	3.27	3.39	3.48	3.56	3.62	3.68	3.72	3.77
24	3.09	3.26	3.38	3.47	3.54	3.60	3.66	3.70	3.75
25	3.08	3.24	3.36	3.45	3.52	3.58	3.64	3.68	3.73
30	3.03	3.19	3.30	3.39	3.45	3.51	3.56	3.61	3.65
40	2.97	3.12	3.23	3.31	3.37	3.43	3.47	3.51	3.55
50	2.94	3.08	3.18	3.26	3.32	3.38	3.42	3.46	3.50
75	2.89	3.03	3.13	3.20	3.26	3.31	3.35	3.39	3.43
100	2.87	3.01	3.10	3.17	3.23	3.28	3.32	3.36	3.39
∞	2.81	2.94	3.02	3.09	3.14	3.19	3.23	3.26	3.29

SOURCE: Adapted from Howell (1987: Appendix t', pp. 590–593)

REFERENCES

BLACK, V. (1955) "Laboratory versus field research in psychology and the social sciences." British Journal for the Philosophy of Science 5: 319–330.

BOX, J. F. (1978) R. A. Fisher: The Life of a Scientist. New York: John Wiley.

BRAY, J. H. and MAXWELL, S. E. (1986) Multivariate Analysis of Variance (Quantitative Applications in the Social Sciences, Vol. 54). Beverly Hills, CA: Sage.

COCHRAN, W. G. and COX, G. M. (1957) Experimental Designs (2nd ed.). New York: John Wiley.

COHEN, J. (1977) Statistical Power Analysis for the Behavioral Sciences (rev. ed.). New York: Academic Press.

DECONCHY, J-P. (1981) "Laboratory experimentation and social field experimentation: An ambiguous distinction." European Journal of Social Psychology 11: 323–347.

FISHER, R. A. (1960) The Design of Experiments (7th ed.). New York: Hafner. (Originally published 1935).

HARCUM, E. R. (1989) "The highly inappropriate calibrations of statistical significance." American Psychologist 44: 964.

HOWELL, D. C. (1987) Statistical Methods for Psychology (2nd ed.). Boston: PWS-Kent.

IVERSEN, G. R. and NORPOTH, H. (1976) Analysis of Variance (Quantitative Applications in the Social Sciences, Vol. 1). Beverly Hills, CA: Sage.

KEPPEL. G. (1973) Design and Analysis: A Researcher's Handbook (1st ed.). Englewood Cliffs, NJ: Prentice-Hall.

KEPPEL. G. (1982) Design and Analysis: A Researcher's Handbook (2nd ed.). Englewood Cliffs, NJ: Prentice-Hall.

KIRK, R. E. (1982) Experimental Design: Procedures for the Behavioral Sciences (2nd ed.). Belmont, CA: Brooks/Cole.

KLOCKARS, A. J. and SAX, G. (1986) Multiple Comparisons (Quantitative Applications in the Social Sciences, Vol. 61). Beverly Hills, CA: Sage.

LOVIE, A. D. (1981) "On the early history of ANOVA in the analysis of repeated measure designs in psychology." British Journal of Mathematical and Statistical Psychology 34: 1–15.

MARASCUILO, L. A. and SERLIN, R. C. (1988) Statistical Methods for the Social and Behavioral Sciences. New York: W. H. Freeman.

MARTIN, M. W. and SELL, J. (1979) "The role of the experiment in the social sciences." Sociological Quarterly 20: 581–590.

MYERS, J. L. (1979) Fundamentals of Experimental Design (3rd ed.). Boston: Allyn & Bacon.

O'GRADY, K. E. (1982) "Measures of explained variation: Cautions and limitations." Psychological Bulletin 92: 766–777.

ROTTER, G. S. and ROTTER, N. G. (1966) "The influence of anchors in the choice of political candidates." Journal of Social Psychology 70: 275–280.

SCHULTZ, E. F., Jr. (1955) "Rules of thumb for determining expectations of mean squares in analysis of variance." Biometrics 11: 123–135.

SELVIN, H. C. (1957) "A critique of tests of significance in survey research." American Sociological Review 22: 519–527.

SPECTOR, P. E. (1981) Research Designs (Quantitative Applications in the Social Sciences, Vol. 23). Beverly Hills, CA: Sage.

WEIR, B. T. (1985) "The American tradition of the experimental treatment of elections: A review essay." Electoral Studies 4(2): 125–133.

WILCOX, R. (1987) New Statistical Procedures for the Social Sciences: Modern Solutions to Basic Problems. Hillsdale, NJ: Lawrence Erlbaum.

Additional References

COHEN, J. (1992). "A power primer." Psychological Bulletin, 112, 155-159.

HOCHBERG, Y. (1988). "A sharper procedure for multiple tests of significance." Biometrika, 75, 800-802.

ABOUT THE AUTHORS

STEVEN R. BROWN *is Professor of Political Science at Kent State University. He received his Ph.D. from the University of Missouri-Columbia, where he studied experimentation under Gary Krause and the late William Stephenson. He is currently involved in research in political psychology, the policy sciences, literary criticism, and the emerging field of human subjectivity.*

LAWRENCE E. MELAMED *is a Professor in the Department of Psychology at Kent State University. He received his Ph.D. from the University of Wisconsin where he studied experimental design under the late David A. Grant. His current research interests focus on the analysis of large data sets in longitudinal research in clinical neuropsychology and in the development of diagnostic instruments in this same field.*